History of Ukraine

A Captivating Guide to the Ancient Crossroads of Civilizations, Enduring Traditions, and Resilient Spirit Through the Ages

Free Bonus from Captivating History (Available for a Limited time)

Hi History Lovers!

Now you have a chance to join our exclusive history list so you can get your first history ebook for free as well as discounts and a potential to get more history books for free!

Simply visit the link below to join.

Or, Scan the QR code!

captivatinghistory.com/ebook

Also, make sure to follow us on Facebook, X, and YouTube by searching for Captivating History.

Table of Contents

Introduction – At the Crossroads of History

The nation-state of Ukraine has a long, complicated, and at times controversial history. Even its founding is often disputed. Some say it all began with the Kievan Rus' who hailed from Scandinavia. However, Russian scholars have long contended that Ukraine was founded by the various Slavic tribal groups of the steppes.

But in truth, the history of Ukraine reaches back even further than that. The ancient Greeks are known to have made settlements in the region, as did the Romans. The lesser known of these early residents of Ukraine were the Khazars. The Khazars were a Turkic group of nomads from the steppes who moved into the region in the 6th century CE. The western half of the Roman Empire had already fallen, and the eastern half, known as the Byzantine Empire, was doing what it could to still hang on. The Khazars set up shop in the meantime and became formidable warriors, as well as traders. They were effectively middlemen, as they were in control of the western marches of the Silk Road.

Just like that long and winding road, the history of Ukraine is full of all kinds of interesting twists and turns, from its first mention by Greek historian Herodotus to the chronicles of the Kievan Rus' to the dissolution of the Soviet Union and the current wars between Ukraine and Russia for the domination of eastern Europe. Ukraine is not just a country with a unique past; it is a country with a unique history. Ukraine is positioned precisely at the crossroads of history.

Chapter 1 – The Earliest of Beginnings

As early as the 7th century BCE, settlers from Greece began to appear on the shores of the Black Sea. The Greeks referred to the forested and mountainous terrain they found just north of the Black Sea as Pontos Euxeinos, which translates as "Hospitable Sea."

They might have called it hospitable, but initially, the Greeks knew very little of this region. For them, the lands north of the Black Sea were full of mystery and intrigue. In the absence of facts, speculation tends to run wild, and soon, the Greeks, who are widely known for their fanciful and exciting myths, had fashioned all sorts of tales about the wild peoples that might inhabit this land.

They also mused that some of their own mythical figures might call this part of the world home. For example, it was speculated that north of the Hospitable Sea was where Achilles, the famed hero from the Trojan War, had ended up. These myths would eventually be faced with cold, hard facts as Greeks began to migrate in larger numbers and set down permanent settlements.

These settlers came from a wide variety of Greek city-states from the Greek mainland, and the reasons for their arrival were just as varied. A significant number of these newcomers were likely refugees seeking a better life from the devastation of war, pestilence, poverty, or a combination of all three. Eventually, the Greeks colonized what would later become the coastal regions along the Black Sea, what we now call

Ukraine. These settlements became gateways of the Greek culture, introducing the Greek way of life to the locals.

The Greeks cast their nets for fish and grew grapes to make wine. They also established trade networks among the neighboring peoples of the region, such as the Scythians of the steppes, the Thracians and Dacians to the southwest, and various forest tribes to the north. They traded cloth, gold, silver, and wine. These items were traded for local goods, such as furs, leather, and grain.

Along with trading goods, the Greeks also exchanged many of their ideas and customs with the local inhabitants that they encountered. Some scholars have gone as far as to point out that this ancient crossroads between the Greeks and the local tribes of the Ukrainian Pontic Steppe presents us with one of the first defining moments of Western civilization.

Greece has often been cited as playing a big role in the formation of Western civilization, with most scholars saying it was the actual cradle and origin of Western civilization. To understand what the ancient Greeks represented as a civilization, it is useful to compare them with the different societies they encountered in the Black Sea region.

The non-Greek locals of the Pontic Steppe of Ukraine provided this striking contrast for the Greeks. They began to better understand what they were and what they were not by observing the non-Greek inhabitants of ancient Ukraine.

Herodotus gives us some idea of this period by way of his account written in the 5th century BCE. It speaks of a Scythian ruler whose name comes down to us as Scylas or Scyles. This ruler had a mother who was of Greek origin. She had a great influence on her son, the future Scythian king. The king even learned how to read and write in Greek. Not only that, but he also had a true love of Greek culture, which was evidenced by the fact that he often traveled abroad to visit and stay in Greek cities.

However, his love of all things Greek proved to be a bit too much since it was found that he was secretly living a double life. He had another Greek wife at a personal residence in the Greek settlement of Olbia(located within modern-day Ukraine). His secret life was found out, and people resented him for it.

According to Herodotus, he was seized and executed by the resentful populace. The fact that Scylas was deposed because of his Greek ways appears to be an outlier as it pertains to the willingness of the locals to accept outside customs. For the most part, they intermingled with Greeks and even intermarried with them without any problem.

The Scythians were an important part of the early development of Ukraine. The Scythians, while not perhaps as cultured as the Greeks, were strong militarily. They were very skilled at riding horses, which was a decided asset on the Eurasian Steppe.

It is believed that the Scythians, who first arrived in the region in the 5th century BCE, were of Indo-European origin. The Indo-Europeans are themselves a fascinating group, and they seem to have been highly influential. They reached a high point just before the start of recorded history, when they fanned out from Europe all the way to India.

The Scythians would eventually become displaced by the arrival of a nomadic people known as the Sarmatians. The Scythians were largely pushed into Crimea, where they formed a much smaller but still fairly robust kingdom that has subsequently been referred to as Scythia Minor.

During this period, Greek colonies along the northern Black Sea coast–places like Olbia, Chersonesus, and Panticapaeum–continued to thrive. These city-states acted as trading hubs between the Mediterranean world and the nomadic cultures of the steppe. They brought in goods such as pottery, wine, and metalwork and sent back grain, fish, and furs.

Depiction of Kore (Persephone) from Panticapaeum.[1]

Meanwhile, the Sarmatians dominated the open steppe for several centuries. They adopted and adapted many of the Scythians' customs but were also known for their own unique warrior culture, particularly the prominence of their female fighters.

The Sarmatians would face off against new warring tribes, such as the Goths and the Huns, in the 3rd century CE. These warring tribes that menaced Ukraine would soon march farther west to Rome itself, where they would help instigate the decline and ultimate fall of the western half of the Roman Empire.

Another group arrived on the scene in the meantime that would play an influential role in this part of the world. That group was known as the Slavs. Although other groups arrived and then eventually passed on to other (perhaps more Roman) pastures, the Slavic peoples decided to set down roots and stay.

Although it is not entirely clear when the Slavic migration first began, it is believed they first became a notable presence around the 6th century CE when they began to deal more with the eastern half of the Roman Empire. The Eastern Roman Empire, which later became known as the Byzantine Empire, managed to survive even after the Western Roman Empire fell.

The Byzantine Empire, rather than being centered around Rome, was centered around the city of Constantinople. This great city was founded by Roman Emperor Constantine the Great in the 4th century CE and would remain a formidable metropolis of Greco-Roman culture until it was overrun by the Ottoman Turks in 1453. It was ultimately transformed into the capital of Turkey, Istanbul.

The Slavic peoples were a diverse bunch and had many branches within their own tribal family tree. Some of the most well known were the Severians, Krivichs, Drevlians, and Vyatichi. The Drevlians, in particular, left us with a wealth of archaeological artifacts. This group was mostly active in the southeastern portions of Ukraine.

There was also the account of 6th-century Byzantine scholar and historian Jordanes, who mentioned the two tribal groups known as Sclaveni and Antes. These two tribes are considered the earliest ancestors of modern-day Ukrainians. These tribes were skilled in the art of war. They might not have fielded large armies, but they had perfected guerilla warfare and certain ambush techniques, which allowed them to take on forces that were normally much larger than their own.

This was during the time of the Byzantine ruler Justinian the Great, who reigned from 527 to 567 CE. Byzantine Emperor Justinian was arguably the most powerful and successful of the Byzantine rulers. He desired to restore the western half of the Roman Empire. Although he never fulfilled this ambition, he came very close, controlling territory in modern-day Turkey, Greece, Italy, the Levant, much of the north coast of Africa, and southern Spain.

According to Byzantine chronicler Procopius, the Byzantines also briefly occupied a portion of Ukrainian territory after defeating the Antes and placing troops just north of the Danube. The occupation was apparently brief. A few years into this occupation, the Byzantines retreated back to the other side of the river. The Byzantines were afraid of spreading themselves too thin. At this point in their history, they were content to defend their borders rather than try to expand them.

Instead, the Byzantines developed what would become their trademark as it pertained to the many nomadic tribal groups that passed through their borderlands. They tried to play them against each other. The Byzantines frequently allied with either the Antes or the Sclaveni and did whatever they could to sow animosity between the two. This was viewed as advantageous because the Byzantines would rather have Slavic peoples of the steppes warring against each other than have them unite and become a much more powerful threat to the Byzantine Empire itself. We are getting ahead of ourselves a bit here, but one could even make the case that the Byzantines eventually sowed the seeds of their own destruction by playing the Turkic tribes of the steppes against each other for so long.

At any rate, the Byzantines would ally with one Slavic tribe of Ukraine when it suited their needs and then turn on them when it did not. In light of this dubious practice, it is really no wonder that the Byzantines frequently earned the animosity of both their enemies and would-be allies. The Slavic tribes of early Ukraine were no different. For example, the Byzantines used the Antes as mercenaries when it was deemed in their best interest to do so. Justinian even repurposed what had been an abandoned city called Turris on the Byzantine frontier. It was located just north of the Danube and would become the headquarters of their new Antes auxiliaries.

The Antes were essentially paid by the Byzantines to be their watchdogs. Over time, though, the Antes wanted more. They were not content just to be paid off; they wanted to become a part of the Byzantine Empire. At one point, they even came up with a scheme to pretend that they had seized a Byzantine general named Chilbudius. They made the absurd claim that the captured general was now their leader.

What was the reason for all this? The Antes felt that being led by a Byzantine general would give them the same status as regular Byzantine soldiers instead of just mercenaries. The plot unraveled when it was found that Chilbudius had been killed and was not with the Antes at all. The Antes were then made to accept the status quo of being foederati, standing watch on the fringe of Byzantine society. (The term "foederati" stems from the word *foedus*, which refers to making an official agreement. Any tribal group that came into an official agreement with the Byzantines was subsequently dubbed "foederati.")

The Antes' role serving as a watchdog for the Byzantines came to an end in the 7th century when a Turkic tribe known as the Avars poured into the region. The Avars were able to overwhelm the Antes, demolishing their foothold in the region. The disruption caused by the Avars would long be remembered. In fact, in the 12th century, Christian Kievan monks reflected on it in their *Tale of Bygone Years*, or as it is otherwise known, the *Primary Chronicle*.

The chroniclers spoke of how unusually brutal the Avars were in their tactics. They also mentioned the Avars' utter contempt for women. These monks talked about how the Turkic Avars seemed to despise women so much that they subjected them to horrendous abuse. Although horses were in abundance, it was said that the Avars made it a common practice to take a group of women and tie them to their horse carts as if they were nothing more than beasts of burden. The women were then forced to pull the conquering Avars around.

If this account is true, it does seem to demonstrate that the Avars were a group who had no compassion or sympathy for those they conquered. The Avars seemed to thrive on not just defeating but also humiliating and degrading their foes in any way they could. They stood out as being absurdly cruel, even during a time period when cruelty in war was common.

Even so, the Avars just might have been too harsh for their own good. Eventually, they infuriated enough people in the region that they all banded together to drive the Avars out for good. The Avars were forced to make way for the next power player of the steppes: the Bulgars. The Bulgars made their presence known in the 7th century. They became foederati of the Byzantines and were allowed to form their own kingdom south of the Danube River.

There was also another Slavic tribe called the Drevlians. The Drevlians were apparently a fairly simple people who dwelled in and around the forested areas in the region. They came into conflict with the Khazars, another group that had migrated into the region after the Bulgars had crushed the Avars.

The Khazars are an interesting bunch. They established a strong state in the region, and at some point, they actually converted to Judaism, marking one of the few times a massive conversion to Judaism occurred in history.

The Khazars were a successful polity while it lasted. They were socially and militarily stable. They also had a great economy, thanks to the control they had established over the important trade routes along the Volga, which led to lucrative trading hubs in the Near and Middle East. Aiding their stability was a treaty that had been established between them and the mighty Byzantines, which occurred sometime in the 620s CE.

The Khazars proved useful enough to the Byzantines, at least at first. They were not only an important hub in the trade network, but they were also a bulwark that stood between the Byzantines and potential antagonists from the Persian Empire and various Arab states, which were coming to prominence at the time.

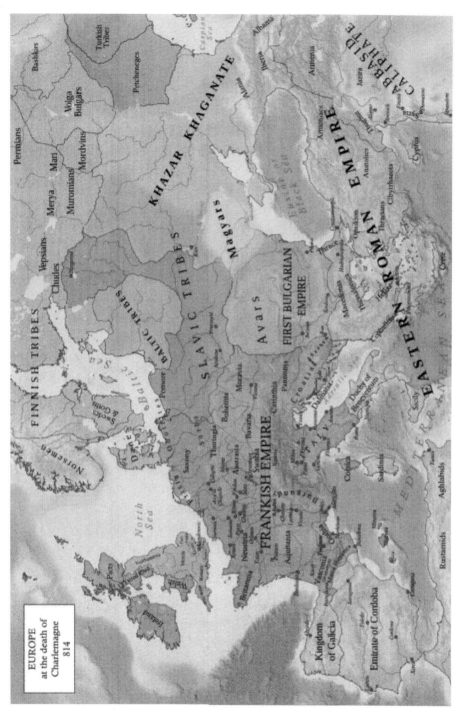

Europe in 814.[2]

In the midst of all of this, many Slavic tribes were gathering in the region. The Kievan chroniclers had much to say about these various peoples, most of it not very flattering. There were accusations made against the Drevlians in particular that cast them as being of the most "bestial" nature. According to the chronicler, this was not as much an exaggeration as an actual fact. He described the Drevlians as being filthy and living just like beasts of the field. They supposedly did not have any qualms with open marriage and just chose anyone they desired on the spot. They also seized food, supplies, or anything else they fancied without any concern for potential repercussions.

It is hard to believe that this was not at least a partial exaggeration. Human beings that entirely devolve into animal behavior could hardly hold any form of society together for long. It stands to reason that the Drevlians must have had their own social rules that held them together as a people, no matter how much others might not have agreed with their social arrangements.

Some of the Kievan chroniclers' claims were later disputed by Ibrahim ibn Ya'qub, a man of Jewish background from Córdoba, Spain. According to Ya'qub, these people were by no means as barbaric as was previously described. For one thing, Ya'qub stated that the marital bonds between men and women of this Slavic tribe were actually very strong. The practice of marital dowries became a major source of revenue among them.

So, there you have it. According to one source, the Drevlians were heathens who practiced bestial and open relationships, yet another contemporary source insists that they loved nothing more than a good wedding. Unfortunately, this divergence in accounts is a troubling but common occurrence when it comes to the history of Ukraine.

When the Slavic confederation known as Kievan Rus' came to prominence, the first semblance of what we now know as Ukraine began to take shape. It is generally believed that after the decline of the Khazar Khaganate, the Kievan Rus' expanded southward into former Khazar territory. The ruler of Kievan Rus', Sviatoslav I, led a campaign against the Khazars in the 10th century, effectively dismantling their power and opening the way for the Rus' to assume control over key trade routes and settlements once dominated by the Khazars.

The location of Kievan Rus'.[i]

This history is still considered complicated and controversial. Although Russian scholars have long insisted that the Kievan Rus' were primarily Slavic in origin, other scholars contend that a large portion of them was of a Norse background, likely coming from Finland.

The Byzantine civilization had already encountered the Vikings by this point. Early Viking explorers had made contact with the Byzantines as early as the 6th century. Many were so impressed with Byzantium that they defected from their own warlords to become mercenaries of the Byzantines.

However, larger numbers of Viking warriors would descend upon the Byzantines and turn decidedly hostile. The capital of Constantinople was actually attacked by a group of marauding Vikings in 860. The attack petered out, and Byzantine Patriarch Photius attributed the respite to the "protection of the Mother of God."[i]

---

[i] Plokhy, Serhii. *The Gates of Europe: A History of Ukraine.* 2015. Pg. 46.

Interestingly, this would lead to a special celebratory feast. The feast never really took root in the Byzantine Empire, but it became very widespread in both Ukraine and Russia when they later became Orthodox Christians. Patriarch Photius himself was actually the one who referred to these marauders as being of the Rus' people.

It is not entirely clear how much these Vikings referred to as Rus' were connected to the later Kievan Rus'. In order to understand the appellation Rus', we have to delve into the origins of the term itself. It seems that the Greeks learned the term from the local Slavic peoples who had, in turn, picked it up from Finish visitors. The Fins were the ones to use the word "Rus'" in reference to their fellow Scandinavians, the Swedes, who hailed from Sweden. It has since been deduced that "Rus'" is likely a derivation of the Swedish phrase *Ruotsi,* which roughly translates to "men who row."[i] Although the term was originally a nickname the Finns had used for the Swedes, it is understandable why just about all Vikings were dubbed as Rus'. After all, the Vikings rowing longboats was a common sight during their incursions.

Patriarch Photius described how the Viking ships swooped down on Constantinople with their crew of men rowing away until they leaped up and exchanged their oars for swords. It is believed that the Vikings might have attacked Constantinople out of anger since the Byzantines had helped the Khazars build a fortress on the left bank of the Don River, which impeded the Vikings' usual trade route.

The Vikings were ambitious traders, but they were not always keen on diplomacy. When they figured out that it was the Byzantines who had allowed their Khazar rivals to get the upper hand, the Vikings decided to send a message to Constantinople.

Their actions ultimately served a twofold purpose since they provided retribution and a chance for plunder. And plunder they did. The Viking Rus' weren't able to break down the walls of mighty Constantinople, but they ran roughshod through what were essentially the wealthy suburbs surrounding the city. They killed anyone who dared to try and defend their possessions and seized whatever they wanted from the populace.

The Byzantines were obviously quite horrified at this event, but such violations of Byzantine territory would continue to become increasingly common as time went on. The Byzantines were apparently able to let

---

[i] Plokhy, Serhii. *The Gates of Europe: A History of Ukraine.* 2015. Pg. 46.

bygones be bygones by 911 CE when the first of several treaties for trading rights were secured between Constantinople and the Rus'.

Another treaty was signed in 944 CE, which was remarked upon at length a few years later by Byzantine Emperor Constantine VII Porphyrogenitus. He wrote on the subject in 950 CE and spoke of, how after this special treaty was made, products from the surrounding Slavic peoples, which were being controlled by the Rus', were traded to the Byzantines. These products were acquired by the Rus' through annual tribute or even force if necessary. It is noted that the Drevlians, in particular, carried out a rebellion against the Rus'.

At any rate, the early Rus' settlers would do quite well for themselves and had a very strong position in the region by the 10th century. The city of Kiev (now known as Kyiv) was their capital. What truly made them political power players was the adoption of Christianity as their official religion in 988 CE. Volodymyr (or Vladimir), Prince of Kiev, came to the throne in 980 CE. He converted and forced all of his subjects to convert as well.

The baptism of the Rus'.'

The conversion of his subjects was by no means guaranteed since being at the crossroads in the region meant the people had multiple options for religion, such as the Norse faith, Islam, and Christianity. Even once Christianity was settled upon as the preferred religion, the Rus' had to choose which branch of Christianity they would follow. The Eastern and Western Churches, although not yet officially split (that would happen in 1054 CE), were divided enough for everyone to know there was a difference between the two.

The people in Catholic Rome wanted the Kievan Rus' to practice Latin rites, while the Greek Orthodox in Constantinople wanted them to follow the Orthodox way of doing things. The *Primary Chronicle* says that when the leaders of the Rus' stepped into the great and impressive monastery of Constantinople, the Hagia Sophia, and partook in all of its splendor, the choice became easy.

One could also argue that sidling up with the major Greek Orthodox power, the Byzantine Empire, only made sense since they were the closest strong Christian ally. Regardless of the reason, the Rus' would indeed choose Eastern Orthodoxy. Both Ukraine and Russia are dominated by the Orthodox Christian Church to this very day.

The Kievan Rus' left lasting monuments to their Orthodox faith, such as the Cathedral of Saint Sophia, which was built in Kiev in 1037. It was based off of Constantinople's Hagia Sophia. The Kievan Rus' sought to bring the majesty of the great Hagia Sophia closer to home. Stained-glass windows and other ornate artwork inside the cathedral tell some of the most famous stories from the scriptures. Powerful imagery like this was considered the most effective means of communicating religious zeal since most of the Kievan Rus' were illiterate at this time. They might not have been able to read the Bible, but it was hoped that after gazing at this architectural marvel, they could come to associate the awe-inspiring wonder it provoked with the majesty of God.

St. Sophia's Cathedral.[5]

The Kievan Rus' would continue to be a major hub of Christian civilization until they were disrupted in the 13th century by the Mongol invasion. The entire trajectory of Ukrainian history would change after the invasion, as life on the Ukrainian steppes would never be the same again.

Chapter 2 – Life under the Mongols

At the behest of the great warlord Genghis Khan, the Mongols poured into the region of Ukraine and subdued the Kievan Rus' by the sword. The Mongols would basically kickstart a new phase in Ukraine's development. Interestingly, as devastating as the Mongol onslaught was in the beginning phase of this conquest, the Mongols actually managed to unify the tribal groups in a way that had not been previously done before.

Prior to the invasion, Ukraine was hopelessly divided into various principalities and territories, with different leaders in charge. This fragmentation was very convenient for the boyars, the Kievan Rus' landowning elite. They wanted control of their own territory, but it hindered any real sense of unity. The Mongols, in their domination of the region, managed to place these lands under one banner, effectively uniting the previously divided and often hostile states, though they were now under foreign rule.

The Mongols first made incursions into the region of Ukraine in 1223 when they clashed with armies of the Kievan Rus' at the Battle of the Kalka River. This battle was inconclusive, though, and the Mongols became distracted by other areas they could conquer.

Genghis Khan also died in 1227, which stopped the conquests for a moment, but his descendants would come to control various sections of the Mongol Empire, referred to as "khanates." Ukraine would eventually become part of what was known as the Golden Khanate or the Golden Horde. This section of the Mongolian Empire originally fell under the jurisdiction of Genghis Khan's grandson, Batu.

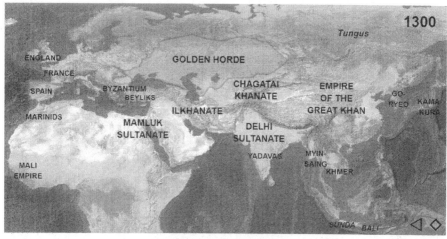

The Golden Horde in 1300.[6]

As ruler of the Golden Horde, Batu sought to make the entire Black Sea region his own personal fief. The first to fall to Batu were the Volga Bulgars. After the destruction of this group, the Mongols went north up the Volga and laid siege to several other villages along the river. The campaign was spectacularly successful, and by 1236, the Mongols were in complete control. After these groups in Ukraine were subdued, Mongol bands began to make forays all the way into Poland, Silesia, and Moravia. The city of Ryazan, the capital of the Ryazan Principality, fell in February 1238. The devastation was so great that only the principalities of Pskov and Novgorod remained intact. The final touches were put in place in the year 1240 when the mighty city of Kiev fell after being sacked by the Mongolian army.

The siege of Ryazan.[7]

The city had been surrounded by the Mongol hordes, and an ultimatum was given to surrender. However, the residents refused to capitulate, so the Mongols rolled out their catapults. The Mongols were experts in early siege warfare, and their powerful catapults, which hurled stone missiles with tremendous force, made short work of the walls of Kiev. After the walls came tumbling down, many people sought refuge in the magnificent Dormition Cathedral. But those seeking safety crowded in so tightly that the foundation shifted, and the whole building collapsed.

Many of those who survived the devastation of the city were hunted down and hounded by the merciless Mongols. Others were able to flee the city and head for the surrounding woods. Here, they initially lived like homeless vagabonds, but over time, they managed to create small settlements in the forested regions of northern Ukraine, which were remote and hidden enough from Mongol eyes to give them some respite.

Not all the people were killed or forced to flee. Some decided to join forces with the conquerors. Certain Kievan Rus' princes, such as Danylo (or Daniel) of Halych, chose to submit to the Mongols, which granted them a degree of autonomy and recognition within the Mongol imperial system. Danylo, however, would eventually switch sides when he believed the moment was right. In 1253, after the pope endorsed a kind of crusade against the Mongols, which involved the armed forces of nearby Hungary, Danylo turned against his former Mongol overlords.

The Mongols were so preoccupied with other affairs in their sprawling empire that they were slow to deliver any payback. In fact, it took five years for a full response from the Mongol forces. Unfortunately for Danylo, the pope's promised crusade never happened. Even though the pope called on various heads of state to participate, no one showed up. Fortunately for Danylo, he was able to talk his way out of this debacle. When the feared Mongol warlord Burundai showed up in his realm, he was able to stay his hand by simply promising to assist him in an invasion of Poland and Lithuania. If Danylo had refused, he would have been easily destroyed, but instead, he became a tool of the Mongols once again. He was forced to attack eastern European nations that otherwise might have rendered him aid. Danylo had been dealt a poor hand, but he tried to play it as best he could.

His situation is remarkably similar to that of Transylvania's Vlad Tepes. Vlad Tepes, also known as Vlad the Impaler or Vlad Dracula, ruled Transylvania during the 15th century. But instead of the Mongols being in control, it was the Ottoman Turks. Vlad Tepes constantly switched sides just to keep his head on his shoulders.

After much bloodshed, the locals of Kiev (those who survived the slaughter anyway) were forced by the Mongols to live under Mongolian dominion. Ironically, they united more after being defeated than they ever would have been had the warring princes of Ukraine been successful in fending off the Mongols.

However, there were certain benefits that the Mongols bestowed upon the subject peoples of Ukraine. For example, the Mongols' methods of warfare were advanced at the time. They were already using gunpowder and, in some instances, even rockets. They also wielded their formidable crossbows when much of the world was still using the much less effective standard bow and arrow. '

Along with introducing better martial techniques, the Mongols also opened the door to trade goods from the Far East. Ukraine was suddenly directly linked to the long and lengthy trade routes that stretched all the way to China. The Mongols also managed to influence much of the arts and even literature that developed in the region. All of these things led to the transformation of Ukraine into a fairly united and unique region.

It was actually around this time that the word "Ukraine" first entered into history. The term is an old Slavic word that means "borderland." There is some dispute on the exact timing of this, but it is widely believed that the term "Ukraine" was already in use by the time of the Mongol invasion and occupation.

Much of modern-day Russia was also under Mongolian jurisdiction. In Russian history, this period, which did not come to an end until the late 1400s, is often referred to as the Tatar Yoke since the region was being ruled by the occupying Tatars. The Tatars were not Mongolian, but they served in the Mongolian armies in large numbers and played a major role in enforcing Mongolian rule. The Turkic-speaking Tatars were the most visible occupiers to the oppressed Russians, so it is understandable why they might have associated them with the oppression they faced under Mongolian occupation.

In the year 1362, after a decisive battle between Mongol forces and a group of Lithuanian and Rus' princes, the Mongols were finally pushed back into the steppes. This encounter, known as the Battle of Blue Waters, took place near the Syni Vody River (also known as the Syniukha River), which today runs through modern Ukraine. The Lithuanian-Rus' army was led by a warrior named Algirdas, Grand Duke of Lithuania. It seems that Algirdas succeeded in defeating the Tatar forces of the Golden Horde, which had been a dominant power in the region. This victory opened the way for the Grand Duchy of Lithuania to become a kind of successor state to the Kievan Rus', with control over large portions of what we now call Ukraine.

The Grand Duchy of Lithuania at its greatest extent.[8]

In 1385, the grand duke of Lithuania, Jogaila, signed what was essentially a prenuptial agreement with twelve-year-old Queen Jadwiga of Poland. The terms of this premarital agreement stipulated that Jogaila would gain the crown of Poland as long as he converted to the Catholic faith. The following year, in 1386, he married the young queen of Poland, uniting the crowns of Poland and the Grand Duchy of Lithuania. This meant that the armies of the two powers were combined, creating a very formidable force. This force was sent to seize the region of Galicia from the Hungarians in 1387, which enlarged their domain even further.

One aspect of the union would create some consternation among the Orthodox faithful since Jogaila agreed to convert to Catholicism, which Jadwiga practiced. This episode is viewed as the start of a centuries-long struggle between Roman Catholicism, which was practiced in Poland, and Eastern Orthodoxy, which was practiced in both Ukraine and Russia. The culture of Poland also had a strong pull on many of the Ukrainian elite or those who wished to become part of the elite since those who made the switch to Catholicism were recognized as *szlachta* (Polish nobility).

At any rate, the Polish-Lithuanian Commonwealth continued to expand, and by the time of the Union of Lublin in 1569, it was very large, encompassing most of modern-day Ukraine.[i]

In the meantime, Russia had begun to shake off the Tatar Yoke. In 1476, Grand Prince Ivan III bared his teeth against the Tatars. Grand Prince Ivan III ruled over what was then called Muscovy, which was centered around the modern-day Russian city of Moscow. In that fateful year of 1476, Ivan III announced his realm as being fully independent and refused to make any further tribute to the Tatar khanate, which had oppressed them for so long. At the same time, he also made it his personal mission to "gather" all of the so-called lands of the Rus'.[ii]

This was, of course, in reference to the traditional stomping grounds of the Kievan Rus' of yore, from which both Russia and Ukraine trace their heritage. Ivan III's ambitions were grand, and soon, he would see himself carrying on the tradition of the great and powerful kings, emperors, and Caesars of old. In fact, Ivan III kickstarted the tradition

---

[i] Plokhy, Serhii. *The Gates of Europe: A History of Ukraine.* 2015. Pg. 83.

[ii] Plokhy, Serhii. *The Gates of Europe: A History of Ukraine.* 2015. Pg. 85.

of referring to Russian rulers as "tsar," which is a Russian variation of the term "Caesar."

Bolstering Ivan III's claims of imperial inheritance was the fact that he had married Sofia Paleologue, a surviving niece of the last Byzantine emperor. Yes, even though that final hold-out of Roman legacy had been crushed by the Turks, Ivan III claimed that he and all of his descendants, through his union with Sofia, were its rightful inheritors.

The Mongols did not take the rejection of tribute lightly, but their final hold on Muscovy slipped in 1480 during the standoff at the Ugra River. No real battle was fought, but the Mongols ultimately withdrew, marking the end of their dominance.

Ivan IV, or as he would otherwise be known "Ivan the Terrible," would likewise claim that imperial inheritance.[i] Ivan the Terrible was very interested in expanding his territory, and he began waging war against what was then called Livonia, which was essentially an amalgamation of Latvia and Estonia.

This kicked off the Livonian War, which ran from 1558 to 1583. This war was not only long but also involved many moving parts, including Poland, Lithuania, Denmark, and Sweden. In between all of this, there was the aforementioned Union of Lublin, which established a single ruler for a Polish-Lithuanian superstate that included much of Ukraine.

In early 1569, Sigismund Augustus, who served as the king of Poland and the grand duke of Lithuania, held negotiations in Lublin, Poland, with one delegation representing the Grand Duchy of Lithuania and another representing the Kingdom of Poland. The meeting began well enough, with both parties coming to an agreement on the establishment of a common king and common parliament while maintaining a certain degree of autonomy for the Grand Duchy of Lithuania.

However, Lithuanian nobles who held large tracts of land balked at the idea of transferring some of their Ukrainian holdings to Polish jurisdiction, which was a sticking point on the Polish side. The Lithuanian nobles actually departed from the discussion, but to their shock, the agreement went forward without them. The Polish-Lithuanian Commonwealth officially came into effect in July 1569, and most of what we now consider modern-day Ukraine was under its control.

---

[i] Hosking, Geoffrey. *Russia: People and Empire 1552-1917.* 1997. Pg. 5.

Chapter 3 – Attack of the Cossacks

During the 15th and 16th centuries, Ukraine experienced a major shift in its political fortunes. The lines were redrawn, and the borders of the region expanded in the eastern and southern frontiers. Studies of linguistic trends show that certain Ukrainian dialects, such as Carpatho-Volhynian and Polisian, spread with this territorial expansion, reaching as far as Stavropol in modern-day Russia. Tracing these dialects is important because it matches the travel of the people who spoke them.

By the 15th century, the Golden Horde had largely been dismantled; only a few splinter groups remained, such as the Khanates of Crimea, Kazan, and Astrakhan. These khanates were largely Muslim and served as satellites to the mighty Islamic powerhouse, the Ottoman Empire, located just to the south. The Ottomans had toppled the Byzantine Empire in 1453 and seized its once glorious capital of Constantinople for their own, transforming it into the city of Istanbul.

Although the Golden Horde's remnants were greatly reduced in power, the fact it had shored up such strong relations with the Ottomans did much to offset their weakened state. The remnants of the Golden Horde actually became one of the Ottoman Empire's suppliers of slaves. The fact that the Ottoman Empire had slaves is something that is often overlooked, but yes, the Ottomans made extensive use of slaves, whether they were for work, pleasure, or as soldiers.

The remnants of the Golden Horde known as the Crimean Khanate became experts at conducting slave raids deep inside the lands of Ukraine. These poor captives were then taken to be sold in the Ottoman markets. Some of these slaves actually found themselves in high positions in Ottoman society. One Ukrainian woman ended up the wife of none other than Suleiman the Magnificent. Suleiman, who reigned from 1520 to 1566, was one of the most dynamic and powerful Ottoman sultans of all, and he was married to a Ukrainian woman named Roxolana. Her son, Selim II, succeeded his father, and under the tutelage of his highly influential mother, he kickstarted major reforms and industrial projects. He even founded Muslim charities for the poor.

However, as spectacular as Roxolana's fate might have been, most of the Ukrainians who were snatched up and sent to the Ottoman Empire were not so lucky. Most were in for a life of drudgery and misery. This misery has long been remembered by Ukrainians, and there are many folk songs that speak of the woes the captives faced, as well as those who dared to try and free them. These freedom fighters were a group of crude but effective men called the Cossacks.

One may naturally ask just who these Cossacks were and where they came from. Scholars believe that they initially were a group of nomads who roamed the steppes. The term Cossack is actually Turkic in origin, meaning "freeman" or "freebooter." This makes sense since the Cossacks were indeed freedom fighters. They were beholden to no one and often conducted raids of their own to free those who had been taken by force.

The Cossacks were a rough and ready bunch who were able to live off the land. They were also highly mobile, which allowed them to quickly get away from larger armed groups. The Cossacks were essentially renegades who played by their own rules. They weren't part of an official nation-state, but in some ways, they operated like a state within a state.

In 1492, the Crimean khan lodged an official complaint to the grand duke of Lithuania, Alexander Jagiellon, citing Cossack raids and even an incident in which the Cossacks had seized a Tatar naval craft. As was typically the case at the time, Alexander and his officials tried to play both sides by making superficial efforts to curtail the Cossacks while sporadically encouraging them to strike out at the Tatars if it suited their objectives.

The Cossacks were used as a kind of advance guard with their settlements that were pushing farther and farther south of Kiev. These settlements often consisted of nothing more than huts. However, as rough as their exterior was, these dwellings were often stuffed with all kinds of stolen loot, and the Cossacks were willing to depart with their goods on the cheap. Fine silk straight off the Silk Road was sold at extremely low rates. By selling stolen goods at low prices, the Cossacks managed to undercut the stranglehold the Ottomans had attempted to secure on trade after the toppling of Constantinople.

Along with raiding the Ottomans, the Cossacks became hired mercenaries when other powers needed them. This was the case during the Livonian War when large numbers of Cossacks.

By 1606, the Cossacks were once again on the rise, tearing a path down the Dnieper and even taking their longboats out into the Black Sea. The Cossacks even stormed Varna, which had long been a stronghold fortress of the Ottomans. They followed up this assault nearly a decade later by tearing into Trabzon. The next year, they were even more daring and made their way down to the harbor of Istanbul (formerly Constantinople), where they laid siege to the harbor and nearby settlements. The Cossacks were so daring and so successful that they provoked fear in the hearts of the Turkish defenders. They also managed to stoke the admiration of nearby Christian rulers who still viewed the Ottoman Empire as the greatest existential threat to Christian Europe.

The Cossacks certainly proved their mettle and soon piqued the interest of Poland. The Polish ended up employing large numbers of Cossacks to serve as auxiliaries in their own army. In the summer of 1620, the Ottomans launched an offensive against the Polish, which included battles against the Poles and a group of Ukrainian Cossacks. It is estimated that the Polish/Cossack forces numbered ten thousand and that the Ottomans outnumbered them approximately two to one.

They fought in the vicinity of the town of Tutora, near what now constitutes the Moldovan-Romanian border. The Polish army lost. This was bad news for Poland since it was inevitable that the Ottomans would follow up this victory by marching on Poland itself. And like clockwork, the next year, an even more formidable Ottoman force, said to number some 120,000 troops, made its way to Poland.

The best the Poles could do was muster a standing army of some forty thousand defenders, of which Ukrainian Cossacks made up a large portion. If ever there was going to be an ultimate showdown between the Cossacks and the Ottomans, this was it. The men battled at the fortress of Khotyn near the Dniester River. Despite their smaller numbers, this Polish/Cossack force put up a tremendous fight.

Ultimately, the battle resulted in a draw. The Ottomans could have pressed further but only at a tremendous cost, so they decided to negotiate a truce. This truce resulted in some territorial loss, but Poland had fought off a large foe and maintained its independence. This happened with no small thanks to the Cossacks. The Cossacks were now in a prime position to be granted special rights and privileges within the Polish-Lithuanian Commonwealth, of which Ukraine was a part.

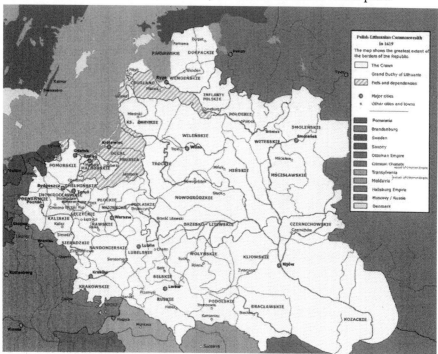

The Polish-Lithuanian Commonwealth at its greatest extent in 1619.[9]

These Cossack veterans demanded the status of nobility, starting with their officers but perhaps eventually extending to all of the soldiers. Such things were not forthcoming, as was proven in 1632 when the Cossacks attempted to attend a meeting of the Polish-Lithuanian Commonwealth's Diet during the election of a new king, only to be shut out from the process.

Unhappy with their situation, the Cossacks lashed out in sporadic uprisings against their benefactors. They staged notable revolts in 1625, 1632, 1637, and 1638. But despite their fury, it seemed that no matter what the Cossacks did, they would remain on the periphery of the commonwealth's society. They were considered useful hands when the time called for it, but they were not considered worthy of any special status within the realm.

Interestingly, in their struggle for acceptance, the Cossacks attempted to use religion to their advantage. The Cossacks appealed to the Orthodox segment of the Polish-Lithuanian Commonwealth instead of the Catholic segment. At first, this tactic seemed to gain some traction, but after reforms were introduced by authorities to give more rights to the Orthodox Church, things changed. The Orthodox population felt secure, so they no longer saw a need to rally behind the Cossacks. As a result, the Cossacks' calls for Orthodox solidarity began to fall flat.

It was not until 1638 that Polish-Lithuanian Commonwealth officials, weary of the turmoil, decided to put forth measures to better acknowledge the role of the Cossacks. They essentially became a separate estate with their own privileges and rights. The Crown created an official registry, and from that point forward, only Cossacks who were on the list were granted legal status and military recognition. Their number was reduced to a quota of around six thousand. Those on the list were granted tax exemptions and land rights in exchange for military service. But those who did not make the cut were pushed back into the ranks of the peasantry.

These efforts only seemed to tide the Cossacks' ambition for a short period. In 1648, an all-out revolt, aptly named the Great Revolt, took place. This revolt was much larger than the previous ones. Unlike the past revolts, which were effectively put down, this popular insurrection proved too difficult for the officials of the commonwealth to subdue. The Poles were then dealt devastating blows at the Battle of Zhovti Vody on May 16th, 1648, as well as at the Battle of Pyliavtsi, which occurred that September.

After this failure to put the revolt down, a Cossack state emerged. This state carved out the boundaries of what we now call Ukraine. In the aftermath of the revolt of 1648 (and several battles and failed treaties later), the Cossack leader (called a hetman), Bohdan Khmelnytsky, paved the way for the formation of the 1654 Treaty of Pereyaslav, which placed Ukraine into the orbit of Russia. Because of the treaty, Cossacks pledged their allegiance to the tsar of Russia.

Bohdan Khmelnytsky.[10]

The Cossacks had already been on the move in Russia, settling far-flung territories in Siberia, and in 1648, they even founded the harbor of Okhotsk. The Treaty of Pereyaslav ultimately sealed the deal of Russian friendship by putting the Cossacks in the pocket of the Russian tsar, who at the time was Alexei Mikhailovich.

On the surface, the tsar claimed that he was aiding the Cossacks in solidarity for their shared Orthodox faith, but on a more pragmatic level, he wanted to use Ukraine as a sort of buffer state against the encroaching Ottoman Empire while also increasing the reach of Russia's imperial footprint. That same year of 1654 saw joint Russian-Ukrainian forces engage in tactical wins against the Poles in Belarus, but revenge was swift. The Poles, aided by Tatar auxiliary fighters, ravaged Ukraine.

The Polish-Lithuanian Commonwealth was beginning to show signs of serious strain by this point. More fighting ensued, which ultimately led to the Treaty of Hadiach in 1658. This treaty was supposed to turn the so-called "Hetmanate" of Ukraine (which had existed as a semi-autonomous Cossack state) into the Principality of Ruthenia.[i] It also stipulated that the Principality of Ruthenia would enter into the commonwealth as a co-equal member with Lithuania and Poland. The treaty granted noble status to many Cossack leaders, which was meant to improve their status in society. Orthodoxy was given official protection, and the treaty even stated that all public offices were to be held by those of the Orthodox faith.

The Russians did not like this agreement because it handed valuable Ukrainian territory to the Polish-Lithuanian Commonwealth. This became a sore spot for the Russians and led to conflict. Relations with Russia broke down so much that a Cossack army faced off against the Russians at the Battle of Konotop in June 1659. The battle proved to be a humiliating defeat for the Russians. They entered into the conflict with some 100,000 troops. By the end, tens of thousands were dead or missing.

Even worse, the Cossack allies, the Tatars, were unleashed and launched raids deep into Russia. The Russians had thought they had shaken off the Tatar Yoke, yet the threat was appearing once again.

However, the Cossacks had their own problem. The Treaty of Hadiach was ratified by the Polish Diet, but it was soon revealed that many of the provisions were not going to be honored.

First of all, the territory allotted to the Principality of Rus had been greatly reduced. Secondly, the Cossack register had been lowered to thirty thousand, which was never agreed to by the Cossacks. This troubling news broke down order among the Cossack ranks. The Cossack leader, Ivan Vyhovsky, was ousted in favor of Bohdan Khmelnitsky's own son, Yurii Khmelnytsky, who took over in the fall of 1659.

Khmelnytsky immediately opened up peace talks with Russia. The Russians confirmed Khmelnytsky's leadership but, at the same time, made him subordinate to Russia. It was agreed that all future elections or appointments would have to go through Moscow. It was also stipulated

---

[i] Plokhy, Serhii. *The Gates of Europe: A History of Ukraine.* 2015. Pg. 129.

that garrisons of Russian troops would be stationed across Ukrainian territory, right in the Cossacks' backyard. This plan was doomed for failure from the beginning, and by 1660, it had broken down completely.

In January 1660, a failed uprising against a Russian garrison near Kiev led to Russian retribution of the worst kind. Khmelnytsky's own cousin, Danylo Vyhovsky, had led the attack on the garrison, only to fall into Russian hands. He was tortured to death, and his body was sent back to Khmelnytsky to send a message.

The body had clear signs of torture. The tsar obviously wanted to scare Khmelnytsky to submit, but the atrocity had the opposite effect. Soon, the Cossacks and the Russians were engaged in open warfare once again. This latest turnaround was as dramatic as it was deadly. In late 1660, the Cossacks were actually fighting for the Russians against Polish troops when Khmelnytsky and his men suddenly switched allegiances right in the middle of battle. Long forced to play one side against the other, the Cossacks suddenly pledged to throw in their lot with the Polish king.

The results were disastrous for the Russians, who suffered a crushing defeat. The constant shifting of allegiances was not good for the Cossacks' long-term goals either, as they now found themselves back in the Polish camp, and the Poles decided to play hardball. They forged a treaty that was even less generous than the Treaty of Hadiach. According to these terms, the Cossacks could not even refer to their territory as the Principality of Rus.

Russia and Poland would come to terms in 1667 with the Truce of Andrusovo. The two parties then went right over the Cossacks' heads by dividing Ukraine between the two of them. According to the new treaty, Ukraine would be divided at the Dnieper River. The territory past the west bank would go to Poland, while the territory past the east bank would go to Russia. The Russian territory included cities like Smolensk and Kiev.

The Russians never really intended for Ukraine to be independent. Russian rulers from here on out engaged in what scholars refer to as the "gathering of the Russian lands."[1] This was basically a process of slowly integrating Ukrainian lands, which the Russians often referred to as Little Russia, into the greater Russian society. Scholars may debate how the

---

[1] Hosking, Geoffrey. *Russia: People and Empire 1552-1917.* 1997. Pg. 25.

geopolitical situation in the region got to this point, but Russia's intention here is quite clear. There was a coordinated effort to keep Ukraine subordinate to Russia at all costs.

For example, in 1686, the Kievan Metropolitanate of the Orthodox Church was made officially subordinate to Moscow. For the religious faithful of the day, this was a big deal. It was just about as big as the Treaty of Perpetual Peace made that same year, which further affirmed Russian dominion over the region.

Chapter 4 – Swallowed up by Greater Russia

By the early 1700s, Ukraine was being swallowed up more and more by Russia, or as Russian nationalists preferred to call it, Greater Russia. Those who were attempting to systematically absorb Ukraine into the Russian state viewed the Ukrainian lands as a subordinate group of territories referred to as Little Russia.

The Cossacks, of course, begged to differ, but they were surrounded on all sides. The hand that they had been dealt was weaker than ever, as was demonstrated in the 1709 Battle of Poltava. During the course of this battle, Tsar Peter the Great waged war against Sweden's Charles XII. The Cossacks were split during this engagement, with some remaining loyal to Russia and others defecting to the side of the Swedes.

The Battle of Poltava.[11]

The Cossack faction that sided with the Swedes was being led by a rather dynamic character: Ivan Mazepa. Ultimately, though, the Swedes were dealt a decisive defeat, which seemed to put the final nail in the coffin as it pertained to Ukrainian independence. Ivan Mazepa would go down in history as the last Cossack leader who seriously attempted to unite eastern and western Ukraine during this age of Russian dominion.

Mazepa had ruled as hetman since 1687, but in 1708, he made the decision to switch sides and join forces with Charles XII of Sweden. After Sweden's crushing loss at the Battle of Poltava the following year, Mazepa fled Ukraine altogether. He made his way to Ottoman Moldavia, where he hid out under the protection of the Turks. He wouldn't live to see what came next. Just a few months later, in October of 1709, he died. Most accounts say he died of natural causes.

Back in Ukraine, things were unraveling fast. The defeat at Poltava didn't just crush the independence movement; it also exposed serious cracks within the Cossack ranks. Some had stayed loyal to Russia, and others had fled with Mazepa. The unity that once defined the hetmanate began to splinter. Moscow saw an opening and wasted no time. Russian troops flooded into the region, and men who would take orders from the tsar were installed.

This would mark the end of Ukrainian ambition for some time, but it kickstarted the beginnings of the great expansion of imperial Russia. In fact, the Battle of Poltava could be said to have established imperial Russia as a superpower.

During this period, Russia sought to expand its reach in all directions, from the east to the west and from the north to the south. The push south had the Russians forcing the increasingly weakened Ottoman Empire farther away from the Black Sea, and the push west rapidly ate into what had been the territory of the Polish-Lithuanian Commonwealth.

Throughout the 18th century, Ukraine was absorbed into Russia. The region of Ukraine and its people would play a big part in Russian affairs from this point forward. During the Russo-Turkish War, which ran from 1768 to 1774, the Cossacks of Ukraine were a vital force that helped achieve a major win for Russia.

This period in western Europe was known as the Age of Enlightenment. However, the situation in eastern Europe was remarkably different. While western Europe struggled over the notions of freedom, equality, and the rights of the individual, much of eastern Europe was fixed in the arms of absolutism. Even so, Russia would have its own supposed "enlightened despot" in the form of Empress Catherine II, better known as Catherine the Great.

Catherine the Great took a fancy to the Enlightenment (she was friends with Voltaire, no less!) while making sure that what was left of the commonwealth was firmly under her heel. For example, she was directly involved in the partition of Poland, which took place from 1772 to 1795.

Russia, as well as Habsburg Austria, would claim much of what we now call Ukraine. It would take until the 19th century for any real semblance of Ukrainian national identity to once again emerge in the consciousness of the Ukrainian people. This loss of cultural identity had been purposefully exacerbated by the policies of imperial Russia. The push for Russification would lead to bans on Ukrainian culture, including the Ukrainian language, which made Russian the lingua franca of the region.

Catherine the Great especially despised the Cossacks and called for them to be banned from office. They were discouraged at every turn. The office of hetman had already been dismantled by Tsar Peter I in 1722, and Catherine tried to finish the job by dismantling Cossack posts. She openly professed her desire to not only get rid of the Cossacks but also to get rid of any memory of them.

In the midst of all of this, Alexander Bezborodko came to prominence. He was born in 1747 and was the son of the general chancellor (what had previously been the post of hetman). Bezborodko was educated at the academy in Kiev.

However, Alexander Bezborodko was not the typical Cossack. After finishing his studies, he enlisted with Pyotr Rumyantsev, who was serving as imperial governor of Little Russia at the time. Bezborodko served with distinction in the Russo-Turkish War, and in 1774, he attained the rank of colonel. In 1775, he was serving at Empress Catherine's court in St. Petersburg.

All of this came close on the heels of the last major Cossack revolt, Pugachev's Uprising, which took place from 1773 to 1775. Although this revolt did not involve territory in Ukraine (it took place in Russia's southeastern frontier), it was the last gasp of any major Cossack resistance to the Russian imperial state.

Massive efforts of what can only be termed "colonization" took place in the wild steppe countries of Ukraine and other areas near the Russian frontier. These settlers were not just from Russia proper; they came from many different locales. For example, Mennonites from Prussia, seeking religious freedom, arrived in 1789, as did German Protestants and Greek Orthodox believers who previously hailed from Turkey. Many more also arrived from the Balkans.

As much as Catherine the Great was for Russification, she apparently did not think that Russians were necessarily needed. Aside from a few skilled Russian officials to train the massive influx of newcomers, the goal wasn't to flood the region with ethnic Russians. The real goal was to bring as many immigrants into the region as possible. Once they were in place, they could be turned into blank slates on which the imperial Russian ethos could be imposed.

Crimea, on the other hand, was another story. Crimea was officially made a Russian possession in 1783. Crimea had long been held by Muslim rulers, so Islam was still a strong force in the region. Here, Catherine the Great tried not to emphasize religion and a general sense of imperial solidarity. She was willing to grant nobility status to landowners who had once thrived under the khans.

Crimea also saw an influx of newcomers, such as Greeks, Italians, Romanians, Germans, or Ukrainians from other parts of Ukraine. With the help of these immigrants, the port city of Odesa was built up on the Black Sea in 1794. Odesa would become one of the most important cities in Ukraine.

Only the far western edge of Ukraine escaped the clutches of Russia since Austria (later Austria-Hungary)claimed this slice of the Ukrainian pie as their own. They would hold onto this possession from 1772 until 1918.

Interestingly, modern-day Ukrainians are likely to point to Austrian rule as a benevolent one. The Austrians were more cosmopolitan, liberal, and accepting in their attitudes, so they are often viewed as helping to keep the flame of Ukrainian identity alive. While this flame was being snuffed out under Russification, the Ukrainians in the far west were allowed to hold on to much of their cultural identity without any major problems.

The western city of Lviv, Ukraine, particularly became a focal point of Ukrainian efforts to maintain their own sense of cultural identity. At the end of World War I and after the fall of the Austro-Hungarian Empire in 1918, this western section around Lviv attempted to declare itself an independent state called the Western Ukrainian People's Republic. But as we will see, this was just a brief reprieve in Ukraine's long history of hardship and oppression.

Chapter 5 – Ukraine during the 19th Century

By the early 1800s, a man named Napoleon Bonaparte had risen to power in France. Napoleon was a French general when the French Revolution broke out. He then rose to the post of first consul in 1799 before being hailed as emperor of France in 1804. Soon after this, the conquering French forces were moving closer to Ukraine.

In 1807, the French troops defeated Prussia. Napoleon then established the Duchy of Warsaw out of the lands that had been previously divvied up in the partition of Poland in an effort to present himself as a liberator. Despite Napoleon's other shortcomings, the Poles could not help but be happy with these developments. When Napoleon launched an invasion of Russia in 1812, the Poles within Russia rose up in large numbers to show their support for the French.

However, interestingly enough, the Ukrainians had a very different reaction to the French than the Poles did. During the course of this struggle, more often than not, the Ukrainians sided with Russia against the French invaders.

Even so, when the invasion was launched in June 1812, Napoleon's huge, battle-hardened army had great potential to defeat the Russians. The Russians, however, had an ace up their sleeve: their unwieldy and expansive terrain. Whether it be Napoleon, Hitler, or some future bold conqueror, anyone who dares to invade Russia has to deal the Russian forces a knockout blow very quickly. Otherwise, the risk of getting bogged down in huge, often frozen, Russian terrain is too great.

Russian generals realized as much during Napoleon's invasion. They utilized tactical retreats, which lured Napoleon and his men deeper and deeper into Russian territory. The Russians also burned everything that would be useful to the French as they moved through the land. From Ukraine to Moscow, everything that the French could use as sustenance or shelter was burned to ashes.

Napoleon was horrified to find that his enemy was willing to seemingly destroy itself in order to prevent him from gaining victory. The tactic was a stunning success. Napoleon and his army camped out in a burned-up and largely deserted Moscow, where they nearly froze to death that winter. The chill became too much for the French to tolerate due to their lack of supplies and proper shelter, and soon, they desperately tried to flee, not from a Russian army but from the Russian winter, as they marched back to France.

And if that was not enough, they were also hunted and harried by the roving Cossacks of Ukraine along the way. The main Russian army would also suddenly come out of hiding and do their best to shoot the French troops as they retreated.

Ukraine played a pivotal role in all of this. Besides providing the firepower of the Cossacks, Ukraine, being the breadbasket that it is, also supplied a lot of grain. Grain from Ukraine was shipped directly to Russian troops to keep them sustained as they carried on the fight.

Shortly after the French Revolution, when the wars of France were first heating up, members of the Public Health Committee cited that Ukraine and its abundance of grain was a vital resource for the Russians. It was predicted that without Ukraine's supply of grain, the Russians' ability to wage war would be greatly diminished.

This French committee also took note that the Ukrainians were bold, noble people who longed for their own independence. Having said that, it is important to acknowledge that not all Ukrainians supported the Russians. Some had come to view Napoleon as a potential pathway to independence. At the beginning of the invasion, Ukrainian Archbishop Varlaam Shyshatsky made a point of publicly supporting Napoleon's efforts. He was, of course, dealt with by the Russians later on for his encouragement of the enemy.

Napoleon had been briefed on the usefulness of Ukraine. He realized that both Ukrainian grain and Ukrainian troops (namely the Cossacks) would be very beneficial to have on his side. He would have loved to have gained both of these assets. As it turns out, though, one of the big deciding factors that ultimately rallied the Ukrainian elite against the French during this period were fears that Napoleon would fold Ukraine into a resurrected Poland.

These fears started to pick up steam after the Grand Duchy of Warsaw became a vassal state of imperial France and laid claim to Ukrainian lands that had once belonged to Poland before the partitions. Napoleon did not state that he agreed with these aims, but he did not repudiate them either. The fact that Poland was in league with Napoleon and that the Poles were openly floating the idea of taking Ukrainian lands was enough to send a shiver down the spines of those who called the traditional lands of Ukraine their home. Once these notions took hold, the Ukrainians decided to fully throw in their lot with the Russians.

Life under the Russians was never a very happy one, and it was not long before discontent once again bubbled to the surface. In 1825, it appeared in the form of the Decembrist Uprising. Although this revolt was primarily a Russian affair (it was by Russians aimed at Russian authorities), there was a notable Cossack element involved. Some Cossack units made use of the kind of fearsome, guerrilla-style tactics that only the Cossacks could deliver. The revolt was put down, but it was just one sign of further unrest to come.

In the 1840s, political protest movements began to stir up once again in Ukraine. One of the leading lights of this movement was an acclaimed poet named Taras Shevchenko. He was born in Ukraine to a peasant family, but he worked his way up the ranks and eventually served at the court in St. Petersburg, Russia. Here, he was able to demonstrate considerable artistic skill and became part of the inner circle of a growing intelligentsia.

Shevchenko went from drawing sketches to crafting poems, receiving great praise for both. His poems would spark something of a Ukrainian revival. A big part of this was the fact that he crafted his poems in the Ukrainian tongue. He spoke the language of the people. Although Shevchenko was fluent in Russian and could have easily written in the arguably more common tongue of Russia, he was convinced that Ukraine needed a voice.

In 1847, he wrote a preface to one of his books in which he elaborated on these feelings at length. He spoke of how the Poles, Czechs, Russians, and so forth were all printing literature in their languages, yet not much was coming from Ukrainians. He felt this was something that had to change.

Of course, Shevchenko's efforts to give a voice to Ukraine were in direct contrast to the active Russification campaign that sought to suppress the Ukrainian language and culture. Yes, simply by printing his works in Ukrainian, Shevchenko was subverting the will of imperial Russia. And he was not alone. Shevchenko was part of a group of Ukrainian culture buffs who dubbed themselves the Brotherhood of Saints Cyril and Methodius. These gifted intellectuals and artists used folklore, literature, and historical data to try and paint a cultural picture of Ukraine in order to restore some sense of national identity. Such things would not go unnoticed by Russian authorities for long, and the crackdown was immediate.

It was amid this backdrop that the widespread revolutions of 1848 took place. These revolts are mentioned in the plural form because revolutionary fervor took hold from France to Russia and many places in between. These revolutions were spawned by intelligentsia who were inspired by the Enlightenment. They desired to dismantle the monarchic structures of old for more democratic governments.

The ideals of the revolution resonated with both Ukrainians and many everyday Russians. The focal point of the 1848 revolution in Ukraine was in Galicia, a region that today makes up the borderlands of Ukraine and Poland. At this time, the region fell under the jurisdiction of the Austrians. On April 19th, 1848, representatives of the revolutionaries delivered a petition to the Austrian emperor. This petition called for the free expression of the Ukrainian language, customs, religion, and other cultural aspects. This was very important because, prior to this, Ukrainian culture had been greatly repressed by the authorities.

The Russian Empire embarked upon big changes and reforms in the meantime, which ultimately led to the abolishment of serfdom in 1861. Serfdom was the practice of forcing peasants who lived and worked on the property of landowners to remain fixed to that land. Although there were some strings attached, these reforms paved the way for the peasants to gain greater mobility. This greater mobility led some to make their way to Ukraine.

Ukraine was in a unique position by the end of the 19th century. It was still divided between the powers of Russia and the Austro-Hungarian Empire, but it was culturally much stronger and more unified than it had ever been before.

Chapter 6 – Ukraine and a World at War

At the turn of the 20ᵗʰ century, Ukraine was an increasingly troubled place. It was plagued by economic hardships and political unrest. Among those troubles was the plague of antisemitism. In the early 1900s, Ukraine had several notable outbursts of violence toward Jewish communities that lived in the region. One particularly terrible outburst occurred in October 1905.

The unrest began as a reaction to the October Manifesto by Tsar Nicholas II, which promised civil liberties but led to widespread demonstrations. Amidst this turmoil, baseless rumors spread, blaming Jews for the unrest. Everyday Russians with no political motive gathered in mobs to attack them. Hundreds of Jews died, and many properties were destroyed. There was no basis for this terrible collective punishment; it was merely a symptom of the overall disease of antisemitism that had been plaguing Russia for centuries.

Ukrainians on both the Austrian and the Russian side of Ukraine had been quite busy in the meantime, trying to establish their own political parties. This was a period of radical thought, and a general desire for change was building up in the region, as demonstrated by the increasing number of demonstrations for various political and social movements that began to erupt in public spaces.

In the Russian-controlled side of Ukraine, the first real political party was established in 1900. This party was mobilized in the Ukrainian metropolis of Kharkiv. Interestingly, around this time, a group of student activists who refused to join the exclusively Russian political parties instead sought to form a socialist, forward-thinking political movement of their own

This political arm was called, quite simply, the Revolutionary Ukrainian Party. This might not have been the first political party in Ukraine, but it was the first to actively change the status quo. The activists for this group immediately planted several cells of resistance within Ukraine and kickstarted a campaign to get the working classes motivated to join forces with them, encouraging them to act on their disenchantment with the status quo.

Along with all of this, they also forged their own publishing initiative and began distributing publications to the masses. Among the tracts circulated was a pamphlet composed by an attorney from Kharkiv, Mykola Mikhnovsky, entitled "Independent Ukraine." In this pamphlet, Mikhnovsky voiced the aims of the revolutionaries. He spoke of how the downtrodden were struggling to rise up and claim their rights. He especially stressed how Ukraine was trying to free itself from the control of outside oppressors. Mikhnovsky went as far as to describe Ukraine's state as being akin to a form of national enslavement. He then went on to give a bit of a history lesson in which he traced the current discontent all the way back to 1654 and the treaty that had been forged with Bohdan Khmelnytsky.

Mikhnovsky contended that the Russians had trespassed against the civil rights of the Cossack officers after that 1654 agreement. Interestingly, previous Ukrainian firebrands Ivan Vyhovsky and Ivan Mazepa both made the same argument back in the 17th and 18th centuries. The real difference was that Mikhnovsky was through with compromise; he was calling for the complete and utter freedom of his people. It has been said that the words issued by Mikhnovsky set the political world on fire and became a major flashpoint in the Ukrainian quest for freedom.

When the Revolutionary Ukrainian Party came to prominence, Mikhnovsky's words really struck home. However, the party would soon face a personal schism over whether or not a newly freed Ukraine should swing toward socialism or nationalism. These were the two main strains of political thought that much of Europe was deciding between at the time.

As it pertains to Ukraine, all of this was conjecture until the outbreak of the 1917 Russian Revolution. Russia had been teetering on the brink for some time, with its tsar and imperial government propped up by ad-hoc decrees that just barely kept everything together.

World War I erupted in 1914, and Russia was on the front lines of the conflict, fighting off the Central Powers, which consisted of Germany, Austria-Hungary, and the Ottoman Empire. Russia's best resource was its manpower, but due to poor equipment, logistics, and morale, Russia's huge army was becoming increasingly unwilling to be led into the meat grinder.

During this discontent, revolutionaries finally managed to storm the Winter Palace and seize power. Russia was taken over by the Bolsheviks in 1917, led by Vladimir Lenin, and they had no stomach for the war the tsar had started. The Bolsheviks quickly negotiated a truce with the Germans. Ultimately, the Germans would be beaten by Russia's former allies, but for the time being, Russia had been simultaneously defeated and transformed.

In the immediate aftermath of the Russian Revolution, Ukraine was cut adrift. Thanks to all of this turmoil and devastation wrought by World War I and the revolution, Ukrainian independence finally seemed like a very real possibility. That previous summer, Ukrainians had established a group of provisional legislators known as the Central Rada. This group became Ukraine's de facto parliament during this time of crisis.

A stalwart of the Ukrainian Revolutionary Party, Mykhailo Hrushevsky, made a promise that Ukraine would be a bastion of freedom and a welcoming place for all. In light of previous persecutions of Jews, he made sure to stress that Jews would be welcome. He also insisted that Poles and even ethnic Russians would have a place in the new Ukrainian state.

Such sentiments were heartwarming, to be sure, but they also had a pragmatic purpose because they helped to bolster the support of the party from all of the left-leaning minorities within Ukraine. Their help was enough to make sure that the Central Rada would be able to take a stand. During Russia's October Revolution, which sealed its fate as a communist state, Ukrainians moved toward independence.

In 1918, the revolutionaries really got to work. While Russia remained in a constitutional crisis, the Ukrainians took the initiative to print out stamps and their own form of currency. They also borrowed historical symbolism to further cement their hold on their own sense of national identity. In particular, they latched onto the symbol of the trident, which had been used on coins by Prince Volodymyr of Kiev during the days of the Kievan Rus'. They also forged a new flag that bore the colors blue and yellow to represent the coat of arms that had long been used in Galicia. These national symbols were meant to invoke the past and unite it with the present, stirring a sense of Ukrainian national solidarity at long last.

However, the path forward would certainly not be an easy one. The biggest problem came when it was realized that the Central Rada was not equipped enough to create a standing army. There were thousands of individuals willing to join up, but the state apparatus to organize them was just not there. And as history has painfully reminded Ukraine, which sits on an open plain right in the middle of often hostile neighbors, a means of defense is a must.

The Russians, in the meantime, were already establishing multiple units of the Red Army, which would soon menace the Ukrainians. Even worse, perhaps, was the increasing dissent within Ukraine itself. This allowed local Bolsheviks to gain steam. The Bolsheviks were angling to create councils, or soviets, within Ukraine. If the Bolsheviks had their way, there would be no need for the Red Army to be sent into Ukraine since they would have turned Ukraine into a Soviet republic from the inside out, as they had done in Russia itself.

When the Central Rada failed to gain proper control of the situation, this seemed like an increasingly likely possibility. In the rural parts of Ukraine, local peasants began seizing land and the means of production on their own. This was right out of the communist playbook of Vladimir Lenin and Karl Marx. Russian communists had cemented their own authority by taking control of these newly created soviet councils.

During the October Revolution, the Russian communists managed to take down the state government in Russia by holding their own special congress in St. Petersburg, which officially approved the soviets (the local councils). The same tactic was attempted in Ukraine with the holding of the Ukrainian Congress of Soviets in Kyiv in December 1917. However, it failed since most of the attendees turned out to be working-class proponents of the Central Rada. The soviets just could not find fertile enough ground in Ukraine to make their schemes come to fruition.

Since they could not seize Ukraine the easy way, they eventually opted for the hard way. In January of 1918, the Red Army was sent in, and in a show of force, they stationed themselves in Kharkiv, which was proclaimed the capital of what was claimed to be the Ukrainian Soviet Republic. Kharkiv is situated near the Ukrainian-Russian border and has always been a hotly disputed territory, just as the headlines of today make so painfully clear.

When the Russian troops poured into Kharkiv, there was very little that the government of Ukraine—the Central Rada—could do about it. Efforts to raise a standing army had been a spectacular failure. Although the Ukrainians of this period were incredibly successful in charting out a path for statehood on paper, unlike their ancestors, who always had formidable militias and warriors at the ready, providing a standing army of any sort seemed to be a very difficult objective to meet.

Unlike the days of the roving Cossacks, the Central Rada was propped up by the intelligentsia and just did not seem to have enough strength to back up all of its intellectual ambition. The intelligentsia in Russia, on the other hand, had successfully roused the masses, and all of the illiterate commoners became fodder for their armies. They did not know too much about Marxist ideology, but they did understand when the communists said they would get their share of land and bread if they picked up their arms and fought for the communists.

Nevertheless, on January 25th, 1918, as much as they were struggling to hold everything together, the Central Rada of Ukraine officially declared its independence as the Ukrainian People's Republic. Along with this declaration, new plans were made to fortify Ukraine's independence by signing peace treaties with Germany and Austria. Germany and Austria-Hungary had not yet been vanquished by the Allied powers. It made pragmatic sense then for Ukraine to try and align with them in an effort to better distance itself from Russia. By doing such a thing, it created the impression that Ukraine was an independent country since only independent countries could make such treaties in the first place. The declaration also expressed Ukraine's desire to live in peace with all of its neighbors, including Russia.

Russia, however, had other plans. It could easily be argued that the only reason Ukraine even managed to get as far as it did in this early struggle for independence was because of how terribly distracted the Russians were by their own internal problems. Once Russia began to somewhat stabilize, it was not long before the Russians began to once again look toward the lands of Ukraine. Little Russia was calling to them once again.

And soon, the Soviet troops were on the march. Not only had they converged on Kharkiv, but they also managed to make it all the way to Kyiv, the capital of Ukraine. They patrolled around the city's northern and eastern sides while communist agitators within Kyiv began to stage revolts and protests. A massive demonstration was held at Kyiv's Arsenal Factory, an important military-industrial complex at the time.

The Central Rada had still failed to bolster its army, and the recruitment drive had apparently fallen flat in light of all of the Russian promises for land and prosperity. The peasantry of Ukraine was promised such things in the beginning, only for the rug to be pulled out from under them later. In later years, Ukraine was subjected to an artificially induced famine at the hands of the communist Russian state.

The peasants might not have understood the specifics, but the grandiose promises alone were often enough to tempt them over to the Soviet camp. Even so, the Ukrainians attempted to rally for their cause. At a railway station in the Chernihiv region, four hundred Ukrainian freedom fighters came to blows with Soviet fighters. After it was all said and done, twenty-seven Ukrainians lay dead. These Ukrainian freedom fighters who gave their lives are known as martyrs in the long march for Ukrainian independence.

The Ukrainians at the time had few options and had to face some rather stark realities. After this engagement, they fled Kyiv and headed for the western edges of Ukraine. Here, they pleaded with the Germans and the Austrians to help them fend off the Russians.

The Germans and the Austrians were running on fumes at this point, but in exchange for the promise of being able to utilize Ukraine's resources, such as grain and raw materials, they had agreed to come to the Ukrainians' aid. They arrived in force on March 2nd and immediately pushed the Soviet Russians out of Kyiv. The task that had seemed impossible for the Ukrainians was apparently easy for the battle-hardened Germans and Austrians.

The retreating Soviets attempted some last-minute diplomacy to hold onto recently installed Soviet enclaves, but the Germans and Austrians pushed them right out and even managed to take Crimea, even though the Central Rada did not recognize Crimea as part of its territory at the time. But now that the Soviets had been driven out, the Ukrainians had new taskmasters to deal with: the Germans and the Austrians.

Chapter 7 – Ukraine's Struggle between the Two World Wars

In 1918, Ukraine found itself between a rock and a hard place. To its east were the armies of Soviet Russia, which very much wished to absorb Ukraine into their new communist government. To the west, the Central Powers of Germany and Austria were in the ascendancy. In this situation, the Ukrainians chose the latter as the lesser of two evils. It was not an easy decision to make, but the Ukrainian leaders of the Central Rada felt they had no choice.

Making matters even more pressing, their new "allies," Germany and Austria, were demanding that they be supplied with one million tons of grain to feed their troops. The Ukrainians were in the process of making good on this demand when the Central Powers abruptly lost patience with the whole arrangement and decided that the revolutionary Ukrainian government needed to be dismantled.

The Germans took the initiative to engineer a new government headed by a Ukrainian general named Pavlo Skoropadski. Pavlo was a descendant of Cossack nobility and was presented as one of the elites of Ukraine's property-owning class. This sort of arrangement was apparently preferable to the Germans than Ukraine's socialist-leaning government that embraced the working class. Ukraine's government was not communist, but for these Germans, socialism was a slippery road to communism, and they preferred to do away with it altogether. They installed Pavlo as their own personal puppet. He ruled as an elitist authoritarian who could only be checked by the Germans and Austrians.

This was certainly not the free, vibrant, independent Ukraine that the Ukrainians asked for. As they say, however, freedom is not free; you have to fight for it. And if you allow someone else to fight for it, as the Ukrainians did with the Germans and Austrians, there is a good chance you might not like the result.

Even though the revolution in Ukraine stalled out and its political trajectory had been significantly altered, tremendous gains to Ukrainian society were still made. Pavlo marshaled the might of modern industry and embarked upon developments of Ukrainian infrastructure. Ukraine saw schools, banks, and government buildings pop up on every corner. Yes, call Pavlo a dictator if you will, but he did get things done. He retooled the Ukrainian army, turning it into a professional fighting force. Ukraine was also gifted with its own national library, an Academy of Sciences, and its own national archives.

One of the greatest advances for Ukrainian national identity was that the Ukrainian language was not only allowed but also encouraged. As harsh as their German and Austrian benefactors were, they had no qualms with the Ukrainians speaking their own language. In fact, they likely preferred they speak it rather than Russian so that they could better disassociate themselves with Soviet Russia.

However, despite these improvements, there was much for Ukrainians not to like. The socialists were, of course, seething with animosity that they had been superseded by this authoritarian regime, and they were not going to let it go any time soon. The working classes resented the fact that the new regime seemed hellbent on working them to death. Since increased production was needed to help supply the Germans and Austrians, the poor found themselves working over twelve hours a day. They worked hard to harvest the bountiful grain, just to see the majority of the fruits of their labor shipped off to foreign troops. This sort of disenchantment with the government led to massive strikes, which only exacerbated the situation even further.

In November 1918, the German and Austrian war effort collapsed, and they were forced to surrender to the Allies, led by America, Britain, and France. An armistice ending the war was signed on November 11th, 1918. As their benefactors crumbled, the authoritarian regime of Skoropadski attempted to do an about-face.

Russia was still fighting an internal battle between its non-communist and communist forces. Skoropadski made the decision to attempt a federalization between Ukraine and the non-communist Russians, creating a new united Russian state in the process. It was a last-gasp effort by a Russian faction that was fading fast, and it didn't hold much promise for anyone involved. It certainly wasn't appealing to the Ukrainians. It was anathema to the ousted leaders from the Central Rada. It would also have long-lasting implications in the future since Skoropadski had essentially attempted to hand over Ukrainian independence.

However, even this bit of desperate grasping of straws was not enough to save Skoropadski's authoritarian dictatorship. The Central Rada regrouped and formed what they referred to as the Directory. It was called as such apparently in a nod to the French Revolution's own revolutionary committee of the same name. Considering the fact that the French Revolution devolved into a horror show of guillotines and mob violence of the worst kind, it makes one wonder why a reference to such a dark period was being made.

Nevertheless, Ukraine's Directory ousted the despot Pavlo Skoropadski. They then cobbled together their own army of sympathetic working-class people and former military men to secure their hold on Kyiv. The Ukrainian People's Republic had returned, and it was now able to take advantage of the modern infrastructure that the hated Pavlo Skoropadski had left behind. They might not have liked Pavlo, but they enjoyed the government buildings that he created.

The next major milestone in the process of Ukraine's postwar independence was the collapse of the Austro-Hungarian Empire. With its collapse, the Austrian-controlled western edge of Ukraine known as Galicia was suddenly up for grabs. Those who lived in the region did not want to wait for someone else to seize their territory, so they made the decision to declare themselves a separate Ukrainian state centered around the city of Lviv.

Perhaps it is not the most creative of names, but this western slice of Ukraine announced itself as the Western Ukrainian People's Republic. Since there was a significant Polish population in the region who believed they had historical ties to the area, this was not an easy task. Shortly after the Western Ukrainian People's Republic had been declared, the Poles attacked. The Poles overcame the Ukrainians and reclaimed the city of Lviv as their own. This forced the government of the Western Ukrainian People's Republic to move their operations farther east as they waged what would become known as the Ukrainian-Polish War. It was a tough time for Ukraine, and the Ukrainians seemed to realize as much, with the two halves of Ukraine, the west and east, decided to come together.

On December 1st, 1918, representatives from both sides of Ukraine declared their intent to merge forces so that they could better survive as a united state. This union was officially announced on January 22nd, 1919. They would try their best to hang on together, even though it seemed that the whole world had somehow come against them.

Ukraine according to a postal stamp.[12]

Once again, the most pressing need of this Ukrainian state was a sound army with which it could defend itself. The union of Western Ukraine (known as the Western Ukrainian People's Republic) was quite beneficial because it provided a group of disciplined and battle-hardened soldiers from Galicia who had served with the Austrians during World War I. After Austria's dissolution, they eagerly signed up to be part of the newly established Armed Forces of Ukraine. Although Western Ukraine had temporarily been made to give up Lviv to the Poles, the rest of Western Ukraine was secure, and the Ukrainian army was being mobilized.

However, the Poles were ready to strike back. They also reconstituted their armed forces, and with a fresh influx of Polish prisoners of war, they ended up fielding an army of some sixty thousand men. This army was sent smashing into Ukraine.

The Poles were actually reprimanded by the French and other Western nations, but the Poles claimed they were fighting Bolshevism, even though the Ukrainians were not actually practicing communism. It is true that the eastern half of Ukraine leaned toward leftist socialism, but they were not communists. Even so, the ideological divide was enough to cause issues, even between Eastern and Western Ukraine. Ideological views even affected perceptions of military discipline. The Western Ukrainians disagreed with the Eastern Ukrainians on how to run military operations, and both began to look toward other powers to align themselves with.

This was a recipe for disaster, and the unity that had been established soon led to chaos and disorder. Scholars point to this period of Ukraine as one of the most chaotic episodes experienced by any country in history. The Ukrainian army was unable to stand against outside forces and was put down. The three main outside antagonists were the Poles, the White Army of Russia, which was fighting Russian communists, and the Red Army of Russia, the military force of the communists.

Between this onslaught of the Poles, the White Army, and the Red Army, the Armed Forces of Ukraine collapsed. Ukrainian society basically collapsed. Citizens fled the cities for the countryside, where they were forced to live off the land by any means possible. Their own conception of civilized society had effectively ceased to exist, and they were made to feel like strangers in what had been their own homeland.

The Red Army won in the long run. The Soviet Russians knew that in order to spread Vladimir Lenin's vision of world domination, they would have to transform Russia into a superstate. The communists were basically aspiring for the Greater Russia of the imperial past, except this time, it would be under a Marxist banner. Russian Marxists knew well enough that Ukraine was key to all of that. Ukraine's abundance of resources, such as coal and grain, would allow Soviet Russia to gain strength and expand its rhetoric to other regions.

So, in the aftermath of World War I, the Soviets were ultimately victorious. They put down the Russian White Army's resistance, consolidated their power, and took over Ukraine. In 1920, Ukraine was being hailed as the Ukrainian Socialist Soviet Republic.

The Soviet Russians were able to co-opt some of Ukraine's socialists. They also managed to galvanize the masses of poor Ukrainians by taking land from landowners and dividing it up among the populace. Through both the stick and the carrot, the Soviet Russians were successful in establishing a firm grip on Eastern and Central Ukraine.

The last real resistance came in the form of Polish armies launching an offensive in April 1920 with the intent of creating a buffer zone out of Western Ukraine, which was situated in between the growing Soviet Union and what was being claimed as part of Poland.

This Polish-propped-up Western Ukraine came into being on May 7th, 1920, with the signing of the Treaty of Warsaw. It was a neutered Ukrainian state, as it had ceded much of Galicia to Poland. It also had an incredibly short life. The Soviet Russians were quick to strike back with a counteroffensive that drove the Polish and Ukrainian forces out on June 13th.

By this point, the Red Army was truly on the march, making considerable gains not just in Ukraine but also in nearby Belarus. At any rate, that bastion of Western Ukraine, Lviv, just like the rest of Ukraine, would soon be in Soviet hands.

Chapter 8 – Soviet Ukraine and the March to World War II

After terrible chaos and struggle, by the 1920s, Ukraine had ultimately been incorporated into the Soviet Union. This meant that the Russian capital of Moscow became the main arbiter of Ukrainian affairs. Any orders given in Moscow were immediately regurgitated in Kharkiv, which had become the Soviet capital of Ukraine or, as it were, the Ukrainian Socialist Soviet Republic.

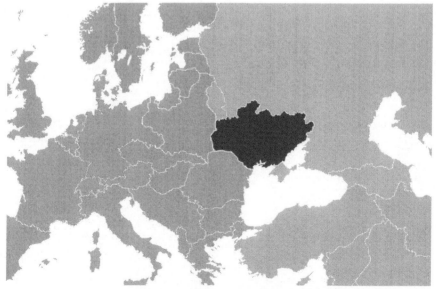

The boundaries of the Ukrainian Socialist Soviet Republic.[18]

It was not a complete loss for the Ukrainians, though. Some silver linings could be found even in this dreadful storm cloud. One thing that Ukrainians could smile about was the fact that, for the first time in quite a long time, Ukraine was a whole and undivided territory (albeit under the control of Moscow). It had clearly defined borders that largely matched the historic boundaries of Ukrainian settlements of the past. It was a Ukrainian soviet republic and part of the larger Soviet Union, but at least the territory of Ukraine had become somewhat defined.

Having this template allowed Ukrainian nationalists to continue to build upon the idea of what nationhood meant for Ukraine. It was done under the shadow of Russia, but the notion of "Ukrainianness" itself was still being considered.

The communists remained on a more or less wartime footing. They were actually engaged in something they referred to as war communism.[i] This was a push to industrialize, nationalize, and militarize all aspects of Soviet control as quickly as possible so that further expansion could be achieved. However, these ambitious efforts had the effect of stripping Ukraine of precious resources that were needed by the Ukrainians themselves.

Inflation began to skyrocket, and there was no perceived end in sight. War communism was supposed to utilize as much as possible from the resources available, but it proved to be a failure. Rather than kickstarting the economy, it crashed it. At this point, it was all anyone could do just to keep their heads above water in Ukraine. In 1921, the production yielded from Ukraine was just one-tenth of what it had been prior to the war.

People were literally starving since they had been reduced to a bread ration of just one hundred grams. Keep in mind that many of these peasants were made to work long hours harvesting the grain, only to barely have enough bread to keep themselves alive. The laboring poor tried to revolt against the impossible conditions that had been inflicted on them, but this just led to even more draconian measures.

Armed guards oversaw many worksites in order to enforce work, quite literally at gunpoint at times. For many Ukrainians, this treatment must have seemed nothing short of a return to serfdom. The grain quotas seemed as if they were destined to continue forever, and the

---

[i] Yekelchyk, Serhy. *Ukraine: Birth of a Modern Nation.* 2007. Pg. 86.

people faced famine. This famine was exacerbated by a terrible drought that hit the region in late 1921. It is estimated that around 235,000 perished during this ordeal, although many scholars believe that the number was likely even higher than that.

Things were so bad that the Soviets had to do what die-hard Marxists considered a complete and utter abomination; they had to appeal to the Western capitalists for help! The United States actually stepped in, footing the bill for a huge famine relief effort. Soviet planners had to acknowledge that their previous efforts had been a failure and returned to more typical market economics. Even private enterprises once again flourished.

In 1924, Vladimir Lenin perished and was replaced by Joseph Stalin. Stalin sought to tamp down the latent feelings of Ukrainian nationalism. In 1929, he had the Soviet secret police infiltrate political groups in Ukraine and had them arrest those who were considered political opponents of the Soviet system. The trials that ensued are largely viewed as complete shams, as their only intent was to engage in the political persecution of any potential opposition.

These show trials were held in Kharkiv and saw several prominent members of the Ukrainian intelligentsia convicted of phony crimes. During the course of the trial, prosecutors tried to make the case that members of Ukrainian political groups were training to link up with the Polish government in efforts to sabotage Soviet policy. Some of the highest profile Ukrainian figures who had their names drug through the mud were the former deputy head of the Central Rada, Serhii Yefremov, and the former Ukrainian prime minister of the failed Ukrainian People's Republic, Volodymyr Chekhivskyi.

Most scholars have claimed that virtually all of these accusations were completely false. Nevertheless, the corrupt judges readily found guilt, and they sentenced 15 souls to their deaths and imprisoned 192 others. Another eighty-seven were sent into exile.

Even though there was a crackdown on those deemed to be politically subversive, the Soviet state made some notable concessions in regard to the Ukrainian language and culture. The communists viewed the Soviet Union as a multinational communist state with Russia at its heart, so they allowed a sort of "Ukrainization" program that helped to offset the previous Russification of the past. Soviet efforts to spread literacy aided this quest, spreading knowledge of the Ukrainian language. Some communists felt that such things would help build a base of power in Ukraine. They felt that if the communists of Ukraine spoke the Ukrainian language, they would be able to attract more people to the cause.

However, as Ukraine entered the 1930s, even the tacit acceptance of some aspects of Ukrainian identity did little to counteract the heavy oppression that Ukrainians felt under the communist regime of the Soviet Union. Stalin himself was not really a fan of Ukrainization. He secretly confided his fear that the Ukrainians would ultimately reject everything Russian, including Leninism.

Over to the west, the rest of Europe was in considerable flux. Germany, in particular, was going through some incredible changes. The Germans had come out on the losing side of World War I and paid the consequences as a result. Despite the fact the Germans had defeated Russia in battle and even occupied Ukraine, their defeat at the hands of the Western Allies had driven them to their knees. They were forced to sign the Treaty of Versailles, which put a high burden of financial reparations on them. They also had to cede territory and trim their military.

The Germans were not happy about any of this and were looking for some way to transform into a more influential power. Unfortunately for them, this transformation came by way of Adolf Hitler and the Nazi Party. Adolf Hitler was made the chancellor of Germany in 1933, and from that point forward, he did whatever he could do to secure power. He was hellbent on restoring Germany as a powerful nation, so he crushed opponents and expanded territorial control. It was not long before Hitler had his eyes on eastern Europe.

Hitler believed that eastern European lands like Ukraine would provide Germany with its so-called *Lebensraum* or "living space." In Hitler's book *Mein Kampf,* he spoke of the results of the 1918 Treaty of Brest-Litovsk, which had the defeated Russians being dictated to by the Germans and Austrians. The result of this treaty gave Ukraine a brief period of freedom right at the tail end of World War I. Hitler spoke of how, although Ukraine was considered independent, it was still occupied by German and Austrian troops and would be a great region for Germany to expand further into.

In the meantime, Ukraine was undergoing yet another terrible famine. This time, though, the famine was, for the most part, artificially induced by impossible grain quotas. This famine, known as the Holodomor Famine, ran from 1932 to 1933 and caused a tremendous loss of life. It's estimated that eighty thousand Ukrainians died in 1932 just around the city of Kyiv.

Starving peasants in Kharkiv.[i]

Local Soviet authorities in Ukraine went on the record to admit that something was wrong. In June 1932, Soviet spokesperson Vlas Chubar publicly acknowledged that the famine was due to "excessive requisitions."[i]

Even so, when complaints reached Joseph Stalin, he mostly ignored them. He even forbade the word famine from being used when talking about the crisis. Stalin was also keen to point the finger elsewhere. In fact, he blamed Ukrainians themselves for much of what had happened.

In August 1932, he wrote a letter to Soviet official Lazar Kaganovich blaming Ukraine's problems on its internal corruption. Stalin seemed to paint a picture of Ukrainian officials being bumbling, inept, and entirely corrupt figures who were messing up the grain quotas and creating the problem themselves.[ii]

[i] Plokhy, Serhii. *The Gates of Europe: A History of Ukraine*. 2015. Pg. 262.

[ii] Plokhy, Serhii. *The Gates of Europe: A History of Ukraine*. 2015. Pg. 263.

Of course, the words of someone like Joseph Stalin, who was quite used to bending the truth if it suited his purpose, should always be taken with a rather large grain of salt. No matter how corrupt Ukrainian bureaucrats might have been, there was no way the famine could be placed entirely at their feet.

The famine did not end because of any sudden act of mercy from the Soviet government. By the second half of 1933, the harvest came in, and there was finally enough food to go around. The Soviets did hand out some food in early 1933, but it wasn't much, and it wasn't for everyone. Meanwhile, grain quotas stayed sky-high, entire villages were blacklisted, and people were barred from leaving in search of food. Even the idea of looking for help was treated like a crime. Millions died, and whole communities vanished. Whatever trust had once existed between Ukraine and Moscow was buried with them.

Stalin stressed to his colleagues that they needed to avoid losing Ukraine at any cost. Stalin was especially worried about Polish designs on Ukraine and sought to bolster Ukraine's defenses from a potential Polish invasion.

This fear of Polish aggression would lead Stalin to sign a non-aggression pact with Germany in August 1939. This pact agreed that the two countries would not attack each other, but it also signed off on a secret plan for both countries to divide Poland between them. According to this secret provision, once hostilities with Poland commenced, the Germans would invade from the west, and the Soviets would invade from the east.

After German troops invaded Poland on September 1ˢᵗ, 1939, Stalin initially delayed any Soviet intervention. He was concerned about being drawn into a broader European conflict, so he hesitated to act. However, under diplomatic pressure from Berlin, which reminded the Soviets of their agreement and hinted that Germany might otherwise take more territory, Stalin ordered the Red Army to invade eastern Poland on September 17ᵗʰ. This move allowed the Soviet Union to secure lands in western Ukraine and Belarus in line with the secret terms of the Molotov–Ribbentrop Pact.

Since Stalin was able to delay his entrance into Poland, he tried to act as if he were merely conducting a military operation to safeguard Ukraine and Belarus from further hostilities that might spill out of eastern Poland. The Western Allies, namely Britain and France, did not really buy this, but they had their hands full with Germany. Luckily for Stalin, they ignored the Soviet invasion and saved all of their firepower for the Germans. For Stalin, this must have initially seemed like a great win. He had managed to seize a chunk of Poland, and Germany was taking all of the blame.

Multiple reasons have been presented as to why Britain and France acted in the way they did. It has been pointed out that the treaty the two powers had with Poland specifically spoke of intervention if Germany invaded, but it did not offer a guarantee in light of Soviet aggression. Beyond this technicality, in a pragmatic sense, Britain and France just were not up for a battle with both Germany and Russia at the same time. They were looking to avoid a fight with Soviet Russia at all costs, so for the time being, they were willing to ignore Soviet aggression.

However, the fates of both Poland and Ukraine were sealed by this series of events. Poland was effectively snuffed out. Two huge armies from two different nations now occupied Poland. The Russians occupied eastern Poland, and they stood between the Germans and their desired *Lebensraum* in Ukraine.

The Germans never intended to keep to their pact with Russia for long. Hitler was looking for the first opportunity to double-cross Stalin and invade farther into eastern Europe.

Ukraine saw the return of Lviv and other parts of Galicia and Volhynia, which had been seized from Poland. This created a much larger Soviet Ukraine. Overseeing much of this was a young Nikita Khrushchev, who had been appointed first secretary of the Communist Party of Ukraine in 1938. Khrushchev actually wanted to expand Ukraine even farther, all the way up to northern Polisia, but this was apparently a bridge too far for Stalin. He opted to incorporate it into Belarus instead. All of this is a clear demonstration of just how fluid the borders of this region can really be.

The Soviets embarked upon a massive deportation campaign of these occupied former lands of both Poland and Western Ukraine. In 1940, a series of arrests took place, with many of the locals being sent to the far reaches of Siberia. By the time the Germans double-crossed the Russians and invaded the Soviet Union in June 1941, some 1.25 million people had been evicted from Poland and Ukraine.

This crackdown created an interesting dynamic in the occupied territories since it led to political dissidents fleeing to the German side.

These individuals would later be used for propaganda purposes and would solidify a trend of Ukrainians supporting Germans as liberators and protectors from the Soviets.

Contrary to popular belief, Stalin had already guessed that Hitler might go back on the pact and decide to invade the Soviet Union. Stalin believed that Hitler might try to double-cross him in 1942, so he was shocked when Hitler ordered the invasion in 1941. However, he should not have been all that surprised because it was the breadbasket of Ukraine that beckoned him to do so.

Hitler realized, just as German war planners of the First World War had surmised, that if a major war was to be conducted across the European continent, major resources would be needed. Hitler felt that Ukraine could supply these much-needed resources. The Germans had since toppled France and seized much of western Europe, but they were faltering in their struggle to knock out Britain. It was determined that the time was ripe to seize Ukrainian resources for the German war effort.

This would bring the Russian bear roaring into the war. Hitler's initial war plans involved charging through Poland and Ukraine, hitting Leningrad, seizing the Donbas (a region in eastern Ukraine), and even taking Moscow itself. The invasion was launched in the early morning of June 22nd, 1941. Germany, along with allied forces from Romania and Hungary, fielded an army that was almost four million strong.

One segment of this force, known as Army Group South, which was stationed in Poland, headed directly into Ukraine. Romanian forces also poured into Ukraine from the south. Aiding them was the dominant German Air Force (the Luftwaffe). It launched a surprise strike on Soviet positions, decimating most of the Soviet aircraft before they could even leave the ground.

The Soviet land army was comparable in size to the Germans and had quite a bit of industrial equipment, such as tanks and artillery. However, the Soviet soldiers were not as disciplined, and even worse, the officers were dreadfully inexperienced. Most of the experienced officers had already been executed, locked up, or deported. These inexperienced commanders often bungled up operations, and some even became so disillusioned that they abandoned their posts.

Considering as much, the morale of the average soldier on the ground was considerably low. Those with perhaps the lowest morale were the Ukrainian troops, who were compelled to fight for the Soviet Union.

Besides poor leadership among their commanders, the Ukrainians had just survived a famine that had largely been foisted upon them by the Soviet regime. They were not exactly the most enthusiastic of warriors that the Soviet Union had at its disposal.

As the Germans continued to gain the upper hand, their morale plummeted to the point that dereliction of duty became second nature. No one wants to fight a losing war, especially for a regime one hates with a passion, so it was quite easy for the Ukrainians to put down their arms and give up the fight.

Before the complete collapse of Ukraine, there was one major counteroffensive that took place in the vicinity of Lutsk, Brody, and Rovno. This involved a push by one of those aforementioned inexperienced Soviet commanders. He basically wanted to throw as many troops and tanks at the Germans as possible in one big push. The only trouble was that the highly mobile and well-coordinated tanks of the German Wehrmacht (the German armed forces) were able to quickly wheel around and encircle the charging Soviets. The Germans were then able to close in and absolutely decimate them.

Even worse was to come. In August of 1941, the Germans seized the city of Uman and took over 100,000 Soviet troops prisoner. The city of Kyiv was captured by the Germans on September 19th, 1941. The prisoner-of-war count was even higher here; it is estimated to have been around 600,000.

Burnt-out buildings in Kyiv.[15]

As mentioned, many at this point were no longer willing to put up a fight, so perhaps this propensity to throw one's hands up into the air and surrender as soon as possible is the most likely reason behind the incredible number of Soviet prisoners of war. The Ukrainians, for the most part, welcomed the Germans as liberators from the hated Soviet regime. This unfortunate fact of history creates much controversy for Ukrainians and has ripple effects that reach all the way to the present day. Because the Ukrainians embraced the Nazis during World War II, it has led critics to characterize Ukrainians as Nazi sympathizers or outright Nazis.

This sort of sentiment (as warped as it might be) was on full display when Vladimir Putin invaded Ukraine in 2022. Putin did not hesitate to poke his finger into Ukraine's painful past by declaring that the Ukrainians were nothing but a bunch of Nazis and that the Russian state was embarking on a military operation to de-nazify all of Ukraine. Most of us may consider such musings absurd, but Ukraine's history of Nazi collaboration enabled Putin and his ilk to make such accusations.

At any rate, the Ukrainians can be given a little slack for their choice to side with the Nazis since most of them likely had no idea what they were dealing with at the time. There were those among them who remembered a much kinder German army that helped Ukraine secure and build up a more modern nation back in 1918. Most had no idea of what Hitler had transformed Germany into. Most Ukrainians thought the Germans were civilized and enlightened western Europeans who would do much to improve the standard of living in Ukraine. In their eyes, almost anything would be better than living under the Soviets.

Some even misunderstood the true meaning of Nazi (the National Socialist German Workers' Party). They believed that the Germans were actual socialists, but they would later learn that the Nazis were determined to dominate the world and implement their own frightening ideology on the people they conquered. The Germans certainly did not have the interests of Ukrainian nationalists at heart and soon made it clear that Ukraine would be a part of their new "living space," taking all of its resources to further the Nazi cause.

The Germans ended up dividing Ukraine into three zones. One was centered around Galicia, another was in Eastern Ukraine, and another was in the south. This latest dismemberment of the Ukrainian state was a clear sign that the Germans were not interested in Ukrainian national solidarity. Those who directly worked with the Germans to help them secure Ukraine soon learned how misplaced their efforts had been.

The OUN (Organization of Ukrainian Nationalists), led by Stepan Bandera, had actually coordinated with German intelligence to form special battalions to aid the Germans during the takeover of Ukraine. These Ukrainian freedom fighters fought alongside the Nazis in the taking of Lviv on June 29th. However, the very next day, they made the fatal mistake of announcing Ukraine to be an independent state. The Germans did not hesitate to turn on their previous comrades. They had Bandera and his inner circle arrested for subverting German interests. Bandera was ordered to denounce his previous declaration.

The Germans likely hoped to achieve a propaganda victory by having a morose Bandera apologize for his efforts for Ukrainian statehood. The Nazis would not get what they wished for; no matter how much he was poked and prodded, Bandera stayed silent. His silence earned him a ticket to Sachsenhausen, Germany, where he was interred in a concentration camp.

Some members of the OUN tried to take advantage of the situation. They toned down their aspirations of nationalism and more closely collaborated with the Nazis. One could chalk this up to the prevalence of corruption among the Ukrainian officials, or perhaps it was pragmatism on their part. After all, Ukraine has a long history of having to play losing hands. Ukraine has been conquered by Vikings, Mongols, Poles, Germans, and Russians. Ukrainian political maneuvering was always rife with having to switch sides at the last minute.

It was not that unusual for some of the more pragmatic card players to try to play the weak hand they had been dealt. However, by 1942, the increasingly belligerent Germans were no longer interested in playing the game at all. The Germans were ready and willing to kill anyone in Ukraine and the rest of the Soviet Union who they deemed expendable.

It has long been noted that while the Germans displayed some modicum of humanity to the Western Allied troops they captured, such as the Americans, British, and French, they were absolutely barbaric toward the Soviet prisoners of war. Many have long marveled at this disparity. Writer and historian Serhii Plokhy has a very interesting theory as to why this might have been the case. He asserts that since Stalin refused to agree to the Geneva Convention of 1929, the Germans exploited this refusal by refusing to grant Soviet prisoners of war the rights and fair treatment outlined in the terms.

By 1942, it was becoming clear to those in Ukraine that the Germans of the Second World War were quite a bit different from the German occupiers who had visited them during the First World War. These Germans were prepared to kill Ukrainians and others on the spot for the slightest perceived infraction.

In truth, the Nazi regime considered Ukrainians as being mostly expendable. The Germans were eager to empty out the land of its current inhabitants so German settlers could move in. It has been said that 60 percent of the prisoners of war taken on the Eastern Front, which included Ukraine, perished while in German custody. Those who were not executed often starved to death. It was certainly a bitter pill to swallow for any Ukrainian who found themselves caught in this terrible trap. They had likely lived through the artificially induced famine of the Soviets, only to starve to death in a concentration camp.

It is true that Ukrainian prisoners were usually treated better than other prisoners of war taken from the Eastern Front, but not by much. One difference was that the Ukrainians were often allowed to be rescued if a family member claimed them. This usually involved a woman claiming that a man was either her husband or son. Since there was no real way to prove such relations, it became common for random women to save men by claiming they were related to them when they were not.

Under the Nazis, Ukraine became a strange and nightmarish place where everyone seemed to be simply doing whatever they could to survive. Thanks to many of the concessions and collaborations that average Ukrainians made, after the war, there was no shortage of Ukrainians with a heavy dose of survivor's guilt.

By 1942, the Holocaust was already in full swing. The horrors of the Holocaust were largely hidden in the concentration camps and inside the gas chambers. In Ukraine, though, mass murder had already been occurring in open sight and often in broad daylight. There were summary executions and mass killings of Jews and other targets of the Nazi regime that Ukrainian locals had to have known about even if they had not outright participated in it.

It is perhaps easy for us to condemn the Ukrainians who stood by and allowed all of this to happen. But to play devil's advocate, they did not have much choice. The Germans had already shown that the slightest sign of disobedience would lead to death or imprisonment. As such, many non-Jewish Ukrainians turned the other way and remained silent during moments of German aggression. It is estimated that at least a million Jews perished in Ukraine, if not more. Unlike other European nations, like France, which made efforts to shield the Jews, the Ukrainians, for the most part, did not provide shelter for their Jewish neighbors. Scholars have since pointed out that many of the non-Jewish Ukrainians who openly collaborated in the killing of Jews had allowed themselves to be brainwashed into believing an antisemitic yarn that had been in circulation for quite some time. This was the false belief that communism was a Jewish ideology. It is true that Karl Marx himself was a Jewish German man, but the correlation between the two is meaningless. To label all Jews as communists simply because Karl Marx was Jewish is absurd. Yet, such things had been common ever since the Russian Revolution of 1917, and there were indeed many in Ukraine who spoke of it all being a Jewish plot.

Nazi propagandists knew about this prejudice among the Ukrainians and sought to exploit it as much as possible. To be clear, a lack of critical thinking is no excuse, but it does seem that many non-Jewish Ukrainians were brainwashed by such beliefs. They had fallen into the trap of dehumanizing the Jews living among them by labeling them as communists. We can shake our heads with disdain at such things today and pretend that they could never happen again, but all one has to do is look at recent headlines to see that history seems as if it is ready to repeat itself. The Israeli-Palestinian conflict, which has picked up steam in recent years, has passionate supporters on both sides, and there is a temptation in both camps to completely dehumanize the other and engage in scapegoating.

This mentality was on display as non-Jewish Ukrainians, alongside Germans, marched Jewish locals into the street. The Jews were beaten, heckled, and laughed at as they were stripped of their clothes and every belonging they had. After this, the victims were shot and shoved into a ditch. These terrible scenes played out over and over again on the streets of Ukraine. At some point, hardly anyone could say that they did not know what was going on. The Jews of Ukraine might not have been transported to the death camps in Poland, but they suffered what many historians have come to call a "Holocaust by bullets."

Although Ukraine was not known for having such camps, writer and historian Serhii Plokhy once described the situation in Ukraine, saying mass murder was ingrained in basically all levels of society. It was akin to a giant, nationwide concentration camp in which everyone was trapped in their own cycles of fear, guilt, and hatred.

Plokhy remarked, "As in the camps, the line between resistance and collaboration, victimhood and criminal complicity with the regime became blurred but by no means indistinguishable." According to him, a German death squad known as the Einsatzgruppen worked alongside local Ukrainian police to apprehend Ukrainian Jews. These Jews were then led to the edge of town, where they were shot and dumped in mass graves.[i]

One of the worst massacres that erupted in Ukraine occurred in September of 1941 in the vicinity of Babyn Yar (also spelled as Babi Yar), where it is believed that well over thirty-three thousand Jewish residents were summarily executed. Both the barbarity and the insidious deception employed during this horrible episode are striking.

Soviet prisoners of war covering up the massacre site.[16]

It all began with leaflets disbursed throughout Kyiv that ordered all Jews to report to a Jewish cemetery in the Kyivan suburb of Babyn Yar. They were told to bring all of their possessions, including their

[i] Plokhy, Serhii. *The Gates of Europe: A History of Ukraine*. 2015. Pg. 280.

documents and even a set of warm clothes. The mention of such things, especially documents like passports and warm clothes, made residents think they were going to be moved to another location. Considering the horrors that they had already faced, this might have seemed like welcome news. However, when they appeared on a Monday morning, on September 29th, near an old Jewish cemetery in Babyn Yar, they were greeted by gun-toting Germans who ordered them to hand over all of their possessions before telling them to strip off their clothes. They were then made to march in groups of ten up a slope overlooking a ravine. They were systematically shot and pushed into the ditch. An entire Jewish community had been slaughtered in a matter of moments. The same thing was later replicated in Kharkiv, where ten thousand Jews were killed.

The Nazi occupation of Ukraine was in many ways much harsher than it was in western European locales, such as Nazi-occupied France, and the retaliation was swift and brutal. Nevertheless, there were some notable attempts to save Jews in Ukraine. The modern nation of Israel has listed over 2,500 citizens of Ukraine who have been deemed as "Righteous Among the Nations" for their efforts to help Jews during the Holocaust. Metropolitan Andrey Sheptytsky of the Ukrainian Catholic Church saved hundreds of Jews in Western Ukraine by hiding them in monasteries and even in his own home.

After the initial onslaught of mass killings, the German occupiers herded Jewish survivors into specially designated ghettos, where they were forced to wear an emblem of the Star of David at all times in order to distinguish their Jewish origin. These ghettos were largely patrolled by the Ukrainian police, who served as auxiliaries of the Nazi regime in Ukraine.

It is said that the worst suffering in Ukraine occurred in the zone near the front called the Reichskommissariat Ukraine. This occupation zone was run by a true tyrant named Erich Koch. Koch was a short, fat, middle-aged man who treated Ukrainians as dogs. He took things to a new level by indiscriminately killing not just Jews but all Ukrainians. By then, those who had looked the other way at the killing of Jews realized that it had become far too late for them to do much about the situation they were in other than pray that the war come to an end.

The Nazis began to be pushed out of Kyiv in the fall of 1943, but they did not fully leave before slaughtering another sixty thousand people at Babyn Yar. This group was a mixture of Soviet prisoners of war, Ukrainian dissidents, Jews, and others. This was a last gasp of wrath by the Nazis, as from here on out, they were pushed farther and farther west by a resurgent Soviet Red Army. The Red Army actually pushed the Germans all the way back to Berlin, where Germany would finally face defeat in May of 1945.

Chapter 9 – The Cold War

Russian troops retook Kyiv on November 6th, 1943, and marched all the way to Lviv by July 27th, 1944. The city of Lviv would cause the most contention since it had been previously seized by the Soviets in the aftermath of the German invasion of Poland in 1939. After World War II came to a close in 1945, the Poles cried foul. They wanted Lviv back.

However, Stalin had outmaneuvered his Polish opponents by getting his own communist agents in Poland to agree with his arrangements. These men were backed up by the Red Army, which had poured into much of central Europe during the later stages of the war. The Poles were forced to form a new state that essentially rendered it a puppet of the communist Soviet Union.

Such things did not occur without a fight, though, and from 1944 to 1947, fierce resistance from underground fighters would continue until the Soviets broke their will to fight.

That same year, there was a population swap. The Ukrainian population in Poland was deported, and Poles were brought in to take their place within the Soviet-defined borders of the newly reconstituted Poland.

The Ukrainians tried to embrace the Red Army troops that poured into Ukraine as liberators, but the Soviets, for the most part, had a hard time believing them. The Ukrainians had welcomed the Germans with open arms—how sincere could they really be? The Ukrainians' hands were also now stained with the blood of complicity and collaboration, which made the situation very complicated.

The fact that a large number of Ukrainians were guilty of aiding German atrocities would leave a lasting legacy in the region. For instance, Soviet authorities had Ukrainians who had lived under German occupation fill out periodic questionnaires for several decades after the war, which quizzed them on their actions during the German occupation. These questions were raised after standard inquiries about one's criminal history.

Clearly, the Soviet Union held Ukrainians in deep suspicion over their actions during World War II. Soviet propagandists also sought to exploit these suspicions and fears by using them to beat down any Ukrainian opposition to Soviet authority. Soviet propagandists especially sought to paint Ukrainian nationalists as Nazi supporters. According to writer and historian Serhii Plokhy, from here on out, if the Soviets had to address an instance of Ukrainian nationalism, they were sure to mention Ukraine's past of Nazi collaboration.[i]

This is all interesting to note since Russian President Vladimir Putin appeared to use the same playbook in the Russian invasion of Ukraine in 2022. He also despises any sense of Ukrainian national identity outside of Russia, and he is quick to call any Ukrainian move toward nationalism nothing short of Nazism. In fact, Putin has described his special military operation in Ukraine as a campaign of denazification.

After World War II, the Soviets expanded their holdings in Ukraine by annexing the Transcarpathian region in what was then called Czechoslovakia. These acts were hailed as the completion of the reunification of Ukraine.

Unlike in other parts of Soviet-controlled regions, which saw religious oppression, the Catholic Church in Transcarpathia was initially allowed to function. It was not until Cold War tensions ratcheted up in 1949 that the doors to Transcarpathia's Catholic Church were closed.

By the 1950s, the witch hunt for Ukrainian nationalists continued, with many losing their livelihoods and others losing their lives. In 1951, the British and Americans backed a secret operation to airdrop pro-nationalist members of the Ukrainian underground, who had been hiding outside of Ukraine, into the region. These secret agents engaged in espionage, collecting intelligence on what was happening on the ground.

---

[i] Plokhy, Serhii. *The Gates of Europe: A History of Ukraine.* 2015. Pg. 297.

The Soviets were outraged to learn of this plot and responded in dramatic fashion. They sent a hitman to Germany, where former nationalist leader Stepan Bandera was hiding. The hitman tracked Bandera down in 1959 and sprayed him with cyanide. The dose of cyanide killed Bandera.

Joseph Stalin had died in 1953, paving the way for his successor, Nikita Khrushchev, to take power. Khrushchev was experienced in matters involving Ukraine, having served there as party leader for many years. His contacts in Ukraine helped secure his grip on power.

Power struggles in the Soviet Union were always an uphill battle and usually involved the jailing or killing of political opponents. Khrushchev was not immune to this. He managed to jail his political opponent Lavrentiy Beriia, the top security tsar, in June of 1953. His next major coup was putting down Stalin's former henchman, Lazar Kaganovich. Khrushchev didn't jail him, but he saw to it that Kaganovich lost influence.

Kaganovich had also been heavily involved with Ukraine in his day. He also had built many strong connections in the region. The fact that Khrushchev was able to put him down so easily has often been chalked up to the fact that he was so close to high-ranking members of the Ukrainian Communist Party.

Ukraine did not go unrewarded. Khrushchev signed away Crimea, making it part of Ukraine's territory. This was done in 1954, but apparently, Khrushchev had suggested doing as much way back in 1944. He had supposedly told Stalin that such a gesture would be a great way of winning over the Ukrainians.

However, since all of Ukraine was part of the Soviet Union, it did not seem to matter too much. Several decades later, though, when Ukraine declared its independence after the fall of the Soviet Union, Russians would rue the day that Khrushchev decided to cede Crimea to Ukraine as a political gift. The fact that Crimea, both then and now, has a majority Russian population only added to the consternation.

At any rate, Khrushchev emphasized elevating Ukraine to more of a junior partner in Soviet affairs, which established Ukraine as a highly influential corner of the Soviet sphere. Many Ukrainian elites were brought to Moscow and placed in key positions of power during Khrushchev's tenure.

Khrushchev openly denounced Stalin in a speech made in 1956. He also criticized much of the way the Soviet Union had been run. To be clear, Khrushchev himself was no saint and would engage in repressive measures of his own. But he did greatly relax the severity of the previous oppression. In some ways, he allowed much greater freedoms in Ukraine. Many writers and artists, for example, had been banned during Stalin's time, but during Khrushchev's reign, they were revived and rehabilitated. Famed Ukrainian poets, such as Maksym Rylsky and Volodymyr Sosiura, were allowed to once again pen their poems in peace.

However, life was still not easy in Ukraine. In the 1960s, famine-like conditions returned. To Khrushchev's credit, rather than exacerbate the situation or use it as an excuse to punish Ukrainian dissidents, he stepped in to help. He actually went as far as to purchase grain from other countries so that it could be used to provide relief to the poor and working classes of Ukraine. Khrushchev definitely had his faults, but he also demonstrated that he had much more of a heart for the average person than Stalin ever did.

Khrushchev eventually fell out of favor in the Soviet Union after the fiasco known as the Cuban Missile Crisis. This was an incident that had nothing to do with Ukraine, but the implications of it and Khrushchev's ouster would have a tremendous impact all the same.

The crisis began after the United States utilized its Central Intelligence Agency (CIA) to orchestrate an invasion of communist Cuba. The invasion force consisted of Cuban exiles who had fled the island after Fidel Castro transformed it into a communist enclave. The exiles were trained and equipped by the CIA in the hopes that they could do America's dirty work of overthrowing Castro without the US being held responsible.

In 1961, after the exiles landed in a region of Cuba called the Bay of Pigs, they were met with a series of devastating failures and were defeated. The Cubans were then able to get to the bottom of the whole thing and realized that the Americans were behind the invasion. The Soviet Union decided to send nuclear missiles to Cuba as a deterrent to prevent any future invasion.

This led to what was arguably the greatest crisis of the Cold War. It was deemed intolerable to have the nuclear missiles of America's leading adversaries being stockpiled so close to home. As such, the United States of America and the Soviet Union suddenly found themselves on the cusp of an all-out nuclear war. Hardliners on both sides were itching to launch the first strike.

Ultimately, however, US President John F. Kennedy and Soviet leader Nikita Khrushchev decided to let cooler heads prevail. After a dialogue was established, they came to a mutual understanding of sorts. Kennedy pledged not to attempt any further invasions of Cuba as long as Khrushchev agreed to remove the missiles. Nuclear war had been avoided.

Some may think that such an achievement would be worthy of celebration, yet many Soviet hardliners were horrified. They felt that Khrushchev had given too much away and appeared soft. This undercurrent of animosity contributed to Khrushchev's removal in October 1964. Khrushchev was replaced by Leonid Brezhnev, who was a hardliner and brought back many of the Stalin-era policies pertaining to Ukraine.

Ukrainian nationalism was again a matter of debate, and Ukrainian intellectuals were easy targets. By the 1970s, another intellectual purge was in the works. This intellectual purge was coupled with a terrible downturn in the Ukrainian economy. From 1966 to 1985, agriculture dropped from a 3.2 percent production rate to just 0.5 percent. Industrial output also crashed from 8.4 percent to 3.5 percent. Ukrainian gas fields were also depleted since they were being feverishly sold to European markets in order to recoup losses from other sectors.

Such developments certainly did not bode well for Ukraine's future, to say the least. Fortunately for Ukraine, change would soon be in the air. On November 15th, 1982, Leonid Brezhnev died. He was succeeded by former KGB Chief Yuri Andropov. Andropov would not live for too long, abruptly perishing in December 1984. He was replaced by the even more short-lived Konstantin Chernenko, who died in March 1985.

After Konstantin's passing, the Soviet Union gained the dynamic leadership of Mikhail Gorbachev. Gorbachev wanted to get rid of the corruption and backward thinking that was causing the Soviet Union as a whole to go into decline. He also sought to stop what has since been described as a conveyor belt of cronyism in its tracks.[i] There would be no more favoritism for Ukrainian elites.

---

[i] Plokhy, Serhii. *The Gates of Europe: A History of Ukraine.* 2015. Pg. 318.

Many average Ukrainians were excited by Gorbachev's new approach, but it still was not hard for this Russian statesman to rub Ukrainians the wrong way. Gorbachev famously visited Kyiv in June 1985, where he made the fatal mistake of referring to the Soviet Union as Russia. One of the most brilliant schemes of the Soviet Union was its name change. After the Russian Revolution of 1917, Russia was transformed into the Soviet Union, which allowed Russia to absorb several surrounding countries without seeming like a colonizer. It was no longer the Russian Empire and its colonies but rather a union of several Soviet republics. Gorbachev referring to the Soviet Union as Russia pulled back the cloth on this little deception.

In the midst of all this, one of the worst nuclear disasters of all time would occur in Ukraine. The nuclear plant in Chornobyl (Chernobyl), Ukraine, suffered from a catastrophic failure, which would later be blamed on the corrupt and inept practices that Gorbachev was trying to tamp down. It would later be learned that many of the technicians at the plant were not following proper procedures. Many of them were likely not qualified to even hold the jobs they had.

Having someone who is inept working as a nuclear technician simply because they greased the palms of leadership is the epitome of corruption, and it came with some rather dire results. Not only was Chornobyl a nuclear disaster, but it was also a blow to Ukraine's push for modernization. It had been hoped that nuclear power would pave the way toward cheap, efficient, and widely available energy.

The incident occurred on April 26th, 1986. The fourth reactor of the plant melted down after a regular maintenance test went haywire. The explosion lifted up a huge cloud of radiation that rained down death from above. The radioactive cloud then moved with the wind and even passed over Kyiv, causing more sickness and contamination. In the immediate aftermath, it is said that some ninety thousand people were evacuated. A stunning three million people were affected.

The ruins of the nuclear power plant.[17]

The fact that the main personnel who ran the reactor were from Russia and that Ukraine had no control over how the plant was run or over how tests were carried out became a major point of criticism. It seemed that Russia had inserted inept technicians into the plant. Even worse, the Ukrainians were the ones expected to clean up the mess. For the most part, Ukrainians rushed into the danger to put out fires and seal off the nuclear power plant. This was no easy task. At least thirty firefighters and other emergency personnel perished in the efforts. Many more would die later from the aftereffects of radiation exposure.

Some wondered why they should even bother trying to correct the errors of the Soviets. Ukrainian intellectuals began to muse about how Russia was trying to dominate Ukraine and how they had used nuclear power as a means of doing so.

Gorbachev's policy of *glasnost*, which means "openness," finally allowed for open criticism of Soviet practices. This opened the door for a tidal wave of complaints, not just over Chornobyl but also over all manner of things going wrong in Ukrainian society. Perhaps most importantly, this new era of openness allowed the Ukrainians to begin the process of opening up about their past history. Ever since the Russian Revolution of 1917, the Soviet state sought to repress, conceal, and alter the facts of Ukraine's history. Now, the chance for a real discussion had presented itself.

The year of 1989 marked a major shift in Ukrainian life. In that year, semi-free parliamentary elections were held. It also marked the start of a major political movement known as Rukh. Rukh transformed into a larger independence movement and would play a pivotal role in Ukraine's break from the Soviet Union.

The Rukh political party was first conceived during meetings held at the headquarters of Ukraine's Writers' Union. These meetings were held in the fall of 1988 and featured writers and other members of the intelligentsia. They met not just to discuss their latest books but also to hammer out ideas of how to make a fairer and more prosperous Ukraine.

That following fateful year of 1989, Rukh had been solidified as a political entity, leading to its first congress in September 1989, in which 280,000 members attended. Initially, Rukh positioned itself as a cheerleader for Gorbachev's reforms and did not really present any kind of political opposition to the Soviet regime. As popular dissent became encouraged under *glasnost*, Rukh began to become a voice of the opposition.

By 1990, Rukh, which then had a membership of around 633,000 people, and other political movements were making the most of *glasnost* and criticizing just about every aspect of communist society. It seems that, depending on their point of view, observers viewed *glasnost* as either Gorbachev's greatest mistake or his greatest triumph. Whatever the case might have been, the wheels were set in motion.

Soon, all corners of the Soviet Union were rumbling with dissent. It was as if people had been living in a dream (or nightmare), and they had suddenly woken up. The Soviet Union was cracking apart at the seams. The Berlin Wall fell down, and the Warsaw Pact crumbled. Soviet satellite states like Ukraine began to pull away from Russia.

Interestingly, just as the mantle of the Soviet Union was about to crack, US President George H. W. Bush paid a visit to Kyiv. The visit was part of a larger trip to the Soviet Union. Bush, who had been carefully watching the steady decline of the Soviet Union, was worried about disorder erupting if the Soviet Union fell apart. His doubts and fears about a post-Soviet world led him to openly downplay, if not discourage, the push toward Ukrainian independence.

During his time in Kyiv, he gave a speech in which he basically cautioned the Ukrainians against making any hasty decisions that could have dangerous outcomes. In particular, he advised Ukrainians not to engage in belligerent nationalism, as it could spell the end of any Ukrainian aspirations for democracy.

Bush was criticized for his discouraging words, but he also had a point, considering the dangers that Ukraine had faced in its quest for nationalism in the past. Belligerent Ukrainian nationalists had made the terrible decision to team up with the Nazis during World War II, so Bush's advice here for pragmatic caution was, in some sense, understandable.

There was also the looming threat of nuclear weapons. Prior to its independence, Ukraine had its own stockpile of nukes. Bush and others were concerned that should tensions ratchet out of control, there could be a nuclear standoff between Ukraine and Russia.

However, Ukrainians seeking independence, freedom, and democracy could not help but feel that Bush's words were a slap in the face. George H. W. Bush came to Ukraine as the leader of the free world and did all he could to prop up the failed policies of the communists.

The Soviet Union disintegrated in December 1991. This paved the way for Ukraine's independence. It had been a long, hard road, but the Cold War was over, and Ukraine was finally free. Considering how short-lived previous instances of Ukrainian independence had been, the biggest question on the minds of most was how long would this remain the case.

Chapter 10 – Modern Ukraine: The Front Lines of World War Three?

After the fall of the Soviet Union and the declaration of Ukraine's independence, Ukrainians sought to reinvent themselves as a viable nation-state. This was demonstrated in the early months of 1992 when most of Ukraine's parliamentary meetings were consumed with coming up with the symbols of Ukraine's independence. During these sessions, the trident from Ukraine's ancient past was made the national symbol, and the colors blue and yellow made up the color scheme of the Ukrainian national flag. An anthem was also established, which is titled with the hopeful yet strangely depressing name "Ukraine Has Not Perished Yet." Since the notion of an independent Ukraine had long been in the works but constantly threatened, perhaps the melancholic title of the nation's anthem is understandable.

More practical matters also had to be addressed, such as what kind of standing army Ukraine would have. The lack of a reliable standing army had plagued Ukraine for centuries. Because of the lack of an armed force, Ukraine had been forced to buddy up with the Germans on two separate occasions. The Ukrainians needed to stand on their own two feet, and in order to do so, they needed their own army.

Ukraine was already home to a Ukrainian Soviet battalion, so they did not have to start from scratch. It was just a matter of converting what they had into a force for an independent Ukraine. This involved the conversion of former Soviet officers into commanders of the Ukrainian army. The army faced a thorough cleaning of its house in the first few months of 1992, and those who could not swear allegiance to the nation-state of Ukraine were out. Around ten thousand people left their posts.

Nevertheless, by the time spring rolled around, Ukraine's complete takeover of an army group of 800,000 soldiers, which had previously been an integral piece of the Soviet apparatus, was complete. This was pragmatism at work since Ukraine needed troops, and these soldiers were not likely to relocate. This feat was overseen by Ukrainian Air Force General Kostiantyn Morozov. He is an interesting character himself, as he hailed from the war-torn Donbas region of Eastern Ukraine and was half Russian, half Ukrainian. Nevertheless, he had sworn his allegiance to Ukraine.[i]

Under Morozov's skilled leadership, those 800,000 troops were effectively retooled for the defense of a sovereign Ukrainian nation. However, the matter of the Soviet Black Sea Fleet was more difficult. Both Ukrainians and Russians played a role in the operations of this fleet, so to which side would all of those naval craft go?

This was a contentious issue and led to extensive talks between Ukrainian President Leonid Kravchuk and the president of the newly christened Russian Federation, Boris Yeltsin, starting in May 1992. The talks dragged on. It was not until 1995 that Russia agreed to hand over at least 18 percent of the ships to Ukraine.

More problems arose when Russian ships refused to leave the port of Sevastopol in Crimea. Even though Crimea was considered Ukrainian territory at this time, the Russians insisted on having a presence at the strategic port since it would be in the national interests of Russia. The two sides ultimately reached an agreement in 1997, which affirmed as much and allowed the Russians to maintain a presence at the port.

The Ukrainians were given a pledge by the Russians that Russia would respect Ukraine's national borders. This was a relief for Ukrainians since Russia had acknowledged that Ukraine was indeed a sovereign nation and that its territorial integrity should not be violated by

---

[i] Plokhy, Serhii. *The Gates of Europe: A History of Ukraine.* 2015. Pg. 333.

Russia or anyone else. Similar promises had already been made when Ukraine agreed to give up its nuclear weapons in 1994. Not only did Russia pledge to respect Ukraine's boundaries as part of the treaty that nixed Ukraine's nuclear arms, but the United States and the United Kingdom also promised to provide security assurances to the independent Ukrainian state. Ukraine craved this security and began deepening its ties with the West.

In 1997, Ukraine signed an official charter with NATO (the North Atlantic Treaty Organization) and even opened up an information center in Kyiv. The most skeptical, hardline Russians were not too pleased with this, to say the least. They likely viewed a NATO "information center" in the heart of Ukraine as nothing short of a Western intelligence-gathering outfit that threatened Russian interests.

Ukraine was also strengthening its ties with the European Union. Ukraine entered into a special cooperation agreement with the EU in 1994. In 1998, this agreement became fully operational. This was troubling news for hardline Russians. The fact that it took four years for the agreement to come into effect is likely due to the fact that the EU knew full well of the ire that they were provoking.

Even though most of the world thought that the Cold War was over, these hardliners were still viewing the world as being on the verge of war, and the notion that Ukraine was becoming attached to a Western bloc like the EU began to ring alarm bells.

In 1994, Ukraine elected a new president, Leonid Kuchma, who would run the country from 1994 to 2005. Kuchma's presidency was a rocky one that had numerous scandals and was plagued by instances of corruption. He had managed to win reelection in 1999 but under some rather dubious circumstances. His main political rival, Rukh leader Viacheslav Chornovil, died in a car accident right before the election. Such things could be mere coincidences, but when they repeat over and over in a country like Ukraine, they sow the seeds of suspicion. There was a suspicion of the government, the justice system, and just about everything one might be told. According to an investigation by the government, Chornovil's death was an accident.

In that same year, 1999, Ukraine's foreign debt reached an astonishing 12.4 billion USD. Half of that debt was beholden to the International Monetary Fund, the World Bank, and Russia. However, by 2000, Ukraine had managed to turn a corner. Due to a crackdown on the most egregious corruption, billions of dollars were saved that would have otherwise gone into the pockets of rich oligarchs. This helped to stabilize Ukraine's economy, and the more even playing field encouraged more legitimate-minded businesses to continue operations. Before the year was out, Ukraine's overall gross domestic product had actually grown by 6 percent. Further reform efforts in 2001 helped to boost revenue even more. The Ukrainian oligarchs, of course, were not fans of all of this corruption busting since state corruption had helped to make them rich in the first place.

Kuchma was in for some real political fallout when a security officer released a recording of private conversations. The most shocking thing caught on the recordings, which took place in late 2000, was Kuchma suggesting that a hit be taken out on journalist Georgiy Gongadze. This was quite shocking indeed because, in November of that year, Georgiy turned up dead. Kuchma was confronted with the tapes in 2001, and he admitted that the recording was of his voice, but he also insisted that the references to Georgiy were either doctored or taken out of context.

Even without the musings of murder, the Ukrainian public was rocked by all of the other things that Kuchma said. He cursed and said all manner of despicable things when he thought that no one of import was listening. This caused even his most ardent supporters to turn on him. Due to all of this resentment, Kuchma decided not to run for reelection in 2004.

Instead, the 2004 election would feature the incumbent prime minister, Viktor Yanukovych, who was supported by the establishment, and his opposition, a man by the name of Victor Yushchenko. (Their names look very similar on paper, but they are two very different candidates.) Yanukovych was supported by the corrupt Ukrainian establishment and was looking toward establishing ties with Russia, whereas Yushchenko was a political outsider who was seeking closer ties with western Europe. Once again, it looked as if Ukraine was deciding to look to the west or to the east.

After the 2004 election came to a close, Yanukovych was declared the winner. However, Yushchenko claimed that the election had been rigged and that widespread election fraud had taken place. It would later be learned that these claims were not without merit. Phone calls would later surface from various Yanukovych staffers that indicated the campaign had tinkered with the state electoral commission's server to alter election returns after the fact. This would explain why, one second, Yushchenko appeared to be in the lead, and then, out of nowhere, Yanukovych eked out a win.

Yushchenko and his supporters knew something was off almost immediately, and they were not going to just sit down and take it. Yushchenko insisted that fraudulent electoral activities had occurred, as well as outright intimidation, which was used to keep his voters from casting ballots on election day. Yushchenko's supporters were under the impression that the election had been stolen, and they took to the streets to protest in large numbers. This protest movement was dubbed the "Orange Revolution."

This massive show of unrest led the Supreme Court of Ukraine to step in and toss out the official results. Another election was held, and Yushchenko was indeed declared the winner. Victor Yushchenko took office in January of 2005. Yushchenko was friendly to the European Union and attempted to align Ukraine with the West.

Viktor Yushchenko.[18]

Yushchenko improved certain aspects of life in Ukraine. He allowed more personal freedoms, such as more freedom of speech and the encouragement of a free press. The economy also did fairly well under his term. Even so, corruption was still a problem. This corruption came to the surface in the 2010 presidential election. Yushchenko had been doling out tax breaks and other deals to the oligarch elites of Ukraine. Both his critics and his supporters were sorely disappointed, and it was enough to drag down Yushchenko's bid for reelection. In a rematch against his previous opponent, Victor Yanukovych, he was soundly defeated.

This time around, there were no charges of election fraud from Yushchenko's supporters. Victor Yanukovych's win was accepted as legitimate. However, it would not be long before unrest would once again surface.

Viktor Yanukovych.[19]

In 2011, Yanukovych sparked international outrage when he orchestrated the conviction and sentencing of his main political rival at the time, Yulia Tymoshenko. Western countries, for the most part, seemed to believe that this action was a politically motivated persecution of a political opponent. This alone was not enough to generate major protests on the streets of Ukraine.

Massive protests did not happen again until President Yanukovych refused to sign the much-anticipated European Union-Ukraine Association Agreement. It seemed as if he was doing the bidding of Russia, which did not want Ukraine to pull closer to the EU. The average Ukrainian proved that they much preferred the West to the East by taking to the streets in huge numbers in late 2013 and early 2014 in what would become known as the "Revolution of Dignity."

This major protest turned into an outright coup, with protesters storming government buildings. Hundreds died during the eruptions of violence. This could have been viewed as an insurrection of sorts, but ultimately, the Ukrainian Parliament sided with the people on the street and voted to pull Yanukovych from his post. It also reversed the conviction and prison sentence of his political opponent, Yulia Tymoshenko. Oleksandr Turchynov was named as the interim president.

Russian President Vladimir Putin keenly observed all of this and made plans of his own. He desired Ukraine to be closer to Russia. If he could not get the whole of Ukraine, he was willing to settle for parts of it. This was made clear on February 26th, 2014, when a group of paramilitary soldiers backed by the Russians burst into the parliament of Crimea and seized control.

A referendum was held that March, in which the Russian-speaking majority voted for Crimea to be returned to Russia. Western officials called foul, but in truth, the Russian majority likely did want to return to Russia. However, the fact that Ukraine had this territory ripped out from under it in this fashion could hardly be called proper. The Ukrainian government did not recognize these developments. There simply was not much that could be done about it at the time.

Russia was not through and began to encourage Russian separatists in the eastern and southern reaches of Ukraine to fight for independence. Putin proposed that regions such as Kharkiv, Luhansk, Donetsk, and

Dnipropetrovsk be incorporated into a buffer state that would serve as a land bridge to the recently annexed Crimea.

The eastern region of Ukraine known as the Donbas had the highest number of and most enthusiastic supporters of Putin's plans. Russian intelligence services worked with these so-called separatists, bolstering their operations and making sure that they continued to be a formidable thorn in the side of the Ukrainian government.

Interestingly, those fighting for the separation of the Donbas and other regions of Ukraine were just as fed up with the corruption and economic disparities. The big difference was that they looked toward Russia to fix their problems instead of Europe. The pro-West and pro-East factions were destined to butt heads, and from 2014 to 2022, they waged a low-level war against each other.

The situation did not really change all that much until February 2022 when Vladimir Putin decided to step out of the shadows. He had long been supporting the insurgents behind the scenes, but now he decided to put his finger on the scale directly. He announced that he would be engaging in a "special military operation" in Ukraine to root out the corrupt, undesirable elements while securing the eastern and southern pro-Russian enclaves.

There were changes in Ukrainian leadership before this happened. Back in May 2014, Ukraine held another election. A businessman named Petro Poroshenko was elected. He had positioned himself as a political outsider who was ready to clean up corruption and get Ukraine back on proper economic footing. However, first, he had to deal with the insurgency in Eastern Ukraine. The Russian-backed separatists had heavier, more deadly weapons at their disposal than the Ukrainian nationalists did.

The Ukrainians needed an influx of arms to help bolster their defense. Unfortunately for them, their Western partners were not so forthcoming. In 2014, US President Barack Obama flatly refused Poroshenko's request for arms and authorized the delivery of only non-lethal aid, which included night vision goggles, blankets, clothing, training, and even counseling for those who had been traumatized by the war. The Ukrainians likely would need a lot of counseling if all they had to beat back Russian tanks was a blanket. The US administration was concerned about escalating the war with Russia, although its hesitancy to aid the Ukrainians more might have negatively impacted the war effort.

It was not until the election of Donald Trump that this situation changed. During the Trump administration, Ukraine was finally given the lethal arms that it craved. In 2017, the Trump administration authorized $47 million worth of lethal aid, including 210 Javelin anti-tank missiles and 37 missile launchers.

Ukraine saw a changing of the guard in 2019 with the election of a popular Ukrainian celebrity by the name of Vladimir Zelensky. President Zelensky was eager to shore up even more support from the United States. At this point, backing the Ukrainians meant helping them fight off Russia's proxies in the country's eastern borderlands.

Vladimir Zelensky.[20]

The game changed in 2022 when Russia outright invaded Ukraine. This kicked off a direct war between Ukraine and Russia. This event occurred under the watch of President Joe Biden. The Biden administration displayed some hesitancy in the opening phases of the war. By 2024, the US had become a vigorous supplier of lethal aid. Over

$180 billion in emergency funding was approved, and tens of billions in military assistance was disbursed to help Ukraine push back against the Russian forces.

However, as of this publication in the spring of 2025, the struggle for the future of modern Ukraine continues to play out. There are ongoing questions about the direction of US policy following the 2024 election, with Donald Trump once again returning to the office of president and signaling a possible shift in American strategy. What happens next remains to be seen.

Conclusion – Ukraine Has Not Yet Perished

Ukraine has long been a point of contention in Europe. Ever since its earliest days when it was a colony of the Greeks, it has been torn between East and West. It was torn between the Slavic tribes and the Scandinavian Viking Rus' and between the Cossacks and the ambitions of would-be imperialists. Ukraine has always been on the front lines of invasion and aggression.

The Mongolian invasion took Ukraine down to its knees. These overlords were shaken off only for Ukraine to be absorbed into a commonwealth of nations. The commonwealth would attempt to hang on to Ukraine until the Russian Empire knocked it loose. Ukraine did not see freedom again until centuries later, at the tail end of World War I.

The Russian Empire had collapsed, and its once mighty grip had finally slipped. The Ukrainian lands the Russians had long referred to as Little Russia were finally free to determine their own fate. This brief window of freedom closed with the rise of the Soviet Union. Soviet Russia would ultimately be the arbiter of Ukraine's fate for the next several decades.

It was only with the end of the Cold War and the dismantling of the Soviet Union that Ukraine once again dared to declare its independence. Ukraine became a free sovereign nation, but Russians were hellbent on recovering Ukrainian territory. They violated Ukraine's borders by launching an invasion. As of this publication, in the early spring of 2025, the war in Ukraine still rages on.

Tanks still smash through defensive barriers, guns fire endless rounds, and missiles rain down death and destruction. Even so, Ukrainians are still rising up to the challenge, and they still sing the words of their national anthem, which declares that the dream for a free and just Ukraine, something desired by all Ukrainians, has not yet perished. For them, the fight for freedom continues.

If you enjoyed this book, a review on Amazon would be greatly appreciated because it would mean a lot to hear from you.

To leave a review:

1. Open your camera app.
2. Point your mobile device at the QR code.
3. The review page will appear in your web browser.

Thanks for your support!

Here's another book by Captivating History that you might like

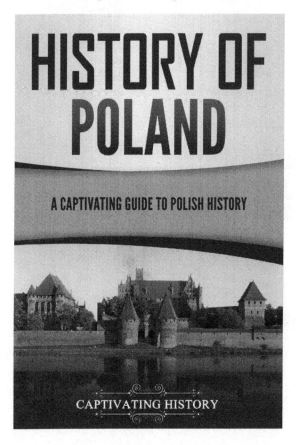

Free Bonus from Captivating History (Available for a Limited time)

Hi History Lovers!

Now you have a chance to join our exclusive history list so you can get your first history ebook for free as well as discounts and a potential to get more history books for free!

Simply visit the link below to join.

Or, Scan the QR code!

captivatinghistory.com/ebook

Also, make sure to follow us on Facebook, X, and YouTube by searching for Captivating History.

Reading and Reference

Hosking, Geoffrey. Russia: People and Empire 1552-1917. 1997.

Plokhy, Serhii. The Gates of Europe: A History of Ukraine. 2015.

Yekelchyk, Serhy. Ukraine: Birth of a Modern Nation. 2007.

Image Sources

1 Carole Raddato from FRANKFURT, Germany, CC BY-SA 2.0 <https://creativecommons.org/licenses/by-sa/2.0>, via Wikimedia Commons, https://commons.wikimedia.org/wiki/File:Fragment_of_a_marble_relief_depicting_a_Kore,_3rd_century_BC,_from_Panticapaeum,_Taurica_(Crimea)_(12853680765).jpg

2 https://commons.wikimedia.org/wiki/File:Europe_814.svg

3 Vitaliyf261, CC BY-SA 4.0 <https://creativecommons.org/licenses/by-sa/4.0>, via Wikimedia Commons, https://commons.wikimedia.org/wiki/File:Location_of_Kyivan_Rus.png

4 https://commons.wikimedia.org/wiki/File:Lebedev_baptism.jpg

5 Rbrechko, CC BY-SA 4.0 <https://creativecommons.org/licenses/by-sa/4.0>, via Wikimedia Commons, https://commons.wikimedia.org/wiki/File:80-391-0151_Kyiv_St.Sophia%27s_Cathedral_RB_18_2_(cropped).jpg

6 https://commons.wikimedia.org/wiki/File:Map_of_the_Golden_Horde_(with_text).png

7 A.N. Mironov, CC BY-SA 4.0 <https://creativecommons.org/licenses/by-sa/4.0>, via Wikimedia Commons, https://commons.wikimedia.org/wiki/File:Defense_Of_Ryazan.jpg

8 CC BY-SA 2.5 <https://creativecommons.org/licenses/by-sa/2.5>, via Wikimedia Commons, https://commons.wikimedia.org/wiki/File:Lithuanian_state_in_13-15th_centuries.png

9 User:Mathiasrex, based on layers of User:Halibutt, CC BY 3.0 <https://creativecommons.org/licenses/by/3.0>, via Wikimedia Commons,

https://commons.wikimedia.org/wiki/File:Polish-Lithuanian_Commonwealth_in_1619.PNG

10 https://commons.wikimedia.org/wiki/File:Bohdan_Khmelnytsky_(Portrait,_sec._half_17th_century,_Chernihiv_Historical_Museum)_(cropped).jpg

11 https://commons.wikimedia.org/wiki/File:Marten%27s_Poltava.jpg

12 https://commons.wikimedia.org/wiki/File:Map_of_Ukraine_(postcard_1919).jpg

13 https://commons.wikimedia.org/wiki/File:Europe_location_UkrSSR_1922.png

14 https://commons.wikimedia.org/wiki/File:HolodomorKharkiv_1933_Wienerberger.jpg

15 https://commons.wikimedia.org/wiki/File:Ruined_Kiev_in_WWII.jpg

16 https://commons.wikimedia.org/wiki/File:Babi_Yar-06-194.jpg

17 IAEA Imagebank, CC BY-SA 2.0 <https://creativecommons.org/licenses/by-sa/2.0>, via Wikimedia Commons, https://commons.wikimedia.org/wiki/File:IAEA_02790015_(5613115146).jpg

18 Muumi, CC BY-SA 3.0 <http://creativecommons.org/licenses/by-sa/3.0/>, via Wikimedia Commons, https://commons.wikimedia.org/wiki/File:Viktor_Yushchenko_2006.jpg

19 The Chancellery of the Senate of the Republic of Poland, CC BY-SA 3.0 PL <https://creativecommons.org/licenses/by-sa/3.0/pl/deed.en>, via Wikimedia Commons, https://commons.wikimedia.org/wiki/File:Viktor_Yanukovych_Senate_of_Poland.JPG

20 President.gov.ua, CC BY 4.0 <https://creativecommons.org/licenses/by/4.0>, via Wikimedia Commons, https://commons.wikimedia.org/wiki/File:Volodymyr_Zelensky_Official_portrait.jpg

Printed in Great Britain
by Amazon

62179535R00060